THE CRUSADES:
A BIBLIOGRAPHY WITH INDEXES

THE CRUSADES:
A BIBLIOGRAPHY WITH INDEXES

JAMES F. MCEANEY (COMPILER)

Nova Science Publishers, Inc.

New York

Senior Editors: Susan Boriotti and Donna Dennis
Coordinating Editor: Tatiana Shohov
Office Manager: Annette Hellinger
Graphics: Wanda Serrano
Book Production: Matthew Kozlowski, Jonathan Rose and Jennifer Vogt
Circulation: Raymond Davis, Cathy DeGregory, Ave Maria Gonzalez and Jonathan Roque
Communications and Acquisitions: Serge P. Shohov

Library of Congress Cataloging-in-Publication Data
Available Upon Request

Copyright © 2002 by Nova Science Publishers, Inc.
400 Oser Avenue, Suite 1600
Hauppauge, New York 11788-3619
Tele. 631-231-7629   Fax 631-231-
E Mail: Novascience@earthlink.net
www.novapublishers.com

#500449923

CONTENTS

PREFACE

Does the end justify the means? Many would argue that the noble objectives of the crusades justified the sometimes ruthless campaigns to achieve them. Others point to the cruelty of some of the crusades as poisoning the purity of the purpose. And still others detest the idea of the crusades in any context. This new book gathers the literature on each of the crusades and provides subject, title and author indexes for easy access.

AUTHOR INDEX

TITLE INDEX

SUBJECT INDEX

BIBLIOGRAPHY

A thirteenth-century minstrel's chronicle: Récits d'un ménstrel de Reims: a translation and introduction / translated with an introduction by Robert Levine. Published/Created: Lewiston, N.Y.: E. Mellen Press, c1990.
Editors: Levine, Robert, 1933-
Description: 134 p.; 24 cm.
ISBN: 0889466238
Notes: Translation of: Récits d'un ménestrel de Reims. Includes bibliographical references (p. 131-134).
Subjects: Romances--Translations into English. Crusades--Romances. Minstrels--France. France--History--Capetians, 987-1328--Romances.
Series: Studies in French civilization; v. 4
LC Classification: PQ1505.R42 A25 1990
Dewey Class No.: 843/.1 20
Language Code: eng fro

Akbar Khan, Mohammed, 1895-
Sultan Salahuddin Yousaf Ayubi versus the crusaders, by Rangrut. Published/Created: Karachi, Islamic Military Science Association, 1968.
Description: xi, 437 p. maps (1 fold.) 23 cm.
Notes: Bibliography: p. 437.
Subjects: Saladin, Sultan of Egypt and Syria, 1137-1193. Crusades. Jerusalem--History--Latin Kingdom, 1099-1244. Egypt--Kings and rulers--Biography. Islamic Empire--History--750-1258.
Variant Series: Islamic ideology on war
Series
LC Classification: D198.4.S2 A6
Dewey Class No.: 962/.02/0924 B

An Old Spanish reader: episodes from "La gran conquista de

ultramar" with introduction, English summary of the chronicle, and etymological vocabulary / [edited by] Vladimir Honsa.
Published/Created: New York: P. Lang, c1985.
Editors: Honsa, Vladimir Jiri Jaroslav, 1921-
Description: 77 p.; 23 cm.
Notes: English and Spanish.
Bibliography: p. 75-77.
Subjects: Saladin, Sultan of Egypt and Syria, 1137-1193 -- Fiction. Crusades--Fiction. Spanish language--To 1500-- Readers. Middle Ages--Fiction. Jerusalem--History--Latin Kingdom, 1099-1244--Fiction.
Series: American university studies.
Series II, Romance languages and literature; vol. 32
LC Classification: PQ6398 .G5 1985
Dewey Class No.: 863 19
Language Code: engspa

Archer, Thomas Andrew.
The crusade of Richard I, 1189-92 / selected and arranged by T. A. Archer.
Edition Information: 1st AMS ed.
Published/Created: New York: AMS Press, 1978.
Description: xi, 395 p.: ill.; 23 cm.

ISBN: 0404154085
Notes: Reprint of the 1889 ed. published by Putnam, New York, in
Series: English history by contemporary writers.
Bibliography: p. [351]-368.
Subjects: Richard I, King of England, 1157-1199. Crusades-- Third, 1189-1192. Great Britain-- History--Richard I, 1189-1199.
Series: English history from contemporary writers.
LC Classification: D163 .A67 1978
Dewey Class No.: 909.07

Armstrong, Karen, 1944-
Holy War / Karen Armstrong.
Published/Created: London: Macmillan, 1988.
Description: xxiii, 452 p., [16] p. of plates: ill. (some col.), maps,; 26 cm.
ISBN: 0333445449:
Notes: Companion volume to the television
Series: The Holy War. "Channel Four book"--Jacket. Includes index. Bibliography: p. 433-440.
Subjects: Crusades. Jihad. Middle East--Politics and government-- 1945- Europe--Relations--Islamic countries. Islamic countries-- Relations--Europe.
LC Classification: D157 .A76x

1988

Armstrong, Karen, 1944-
  Holy war: the Crusades and their
  impact on today's world / Karen
  Armstrong.
  Edition Information: 1st Anchor
  Books ed.
  Published/Created: New York:
  Anchor Books, 1992.
  Description: xviii, 628 p.: ill.; 24
  cm.
  ISBN: 0385241941:
  Notes: Includes bibliographical
  references and index.
  Subjects: Crusades. Crusades--
  Influence.
  LC Classification: D157 .A76
  1992
  Dewey Class No.: 909.07 20

Armstrong, Karen, 1944-
  Holy war: the Crusades and their
  impact on today's world / Karen
  Armstrong.
  Edition Information: 1st ed. in the
  U.S.A.
  Published/Created: New York:
  Doubleday, c1991.
  Description: xviii, 628 p.: maps;
  25 cm.
  ISBN: 0385241933:
  Notes: Includes bibliographical
  references (p. [601]-610) and
  index.
  Subjects: Crusades. Crusades--
  Influence.

LC Classification: D157 .A76
1991
Dewey Class No.: 909.07 20

Armstrong, Timothy J.
  Walter and the resurrection of G:
  a novel and two appendices / T.J.
  Armstrong.
  Published/Created: London:
  Headline, c1995.
  Description: 442 p.; 24 cm.
  ISBN: 0747214190
  Subjects: College teachers--
  Fiction. Manuscripts, Medieval--
  Editing--Fiction. Occultists--
  Fiction. Crusades--Fiction.
  Oxford (England)--Fiction.
  Genre/Form: Detective and
  mystery stories. Occult fiction.
  LC Classification: PR6051.R614
  W3 1995
  Dewey Class No.: 823/.914 21

Atiya, Aziz Suryal, 1898-
  Crusade, commerce, and culture
  [by] Aziz S. Atiya.
  Published/Created: Gloucester,
  Mass., P. Smith, 1969 [c1962]
  Description: 280 p. maps (2 fold.)
  21 cm.
  Notes: "Companion volume to
  [the author's] The crusade:
  historiography and bibliography."
  Bibliography: p. [262]-269.
  Subjects: Crusades. Commerce--
  History--Medieval, 500-1500.
  Civilization, Medieval.

LC Classification: D160 .A8 1969
Dewey Class No.: 940.1/8

Atiya, Aziz Suryal, 1898-
Crusade, commerce, and culture.
Published/Created: Bloomington, Indiana University Press, 1962.
Description: 280 p. maps (2 fold.) 21 cm.
Notes: "Companion volume to [the author's] The crusade: historiography and bibliography."
Bibliography: p. [262]-269.
Subjects: Crusades.
LC Classification: D160 .A8
Dewey Class No.: 940.18

Atiya, Aziz Suryal, 1898-
The crusade in the later Middle Ages, by Aziz S. Atiya.
Edition Information: 2d ed.
Published/Created: New York, Kraus Reprint Co., 1970.
Description: xvi, 604 p. illus., maps. 24 cm.
Notes: Reprint of the 1965 ed. Bibliography: p. 537-570h.
Subjects: Crusades--Later, 13th, 14th and 15th centuries.
LC Classification: D171 .A88 1970
Dewey Class No.: 909.07

Atiya, Aziz Suryal, 1898-
The crusade in the later Middle Ages, by Aziz S. Atiya.

Published/Created: London, Methuen [1938]
Description: xvi, 604 p. illus., maps. 23 cm.
Notes: Bibliography: p. 537-569.
Subjects: Crusades--Later, 13th, 14th, and 15th centuries. Middle Ages--History. Pilgrims and pilgrimages. Islamic Empire--History.
LC Classification: D202 .A8
Dewey Class No.: 909.07

Atiya, Aziz Suryal, 1898-
The crusade of Nicopolis / by Aziz Suryal Atiya.
Edition Information: 1st AMS ed.
Published/Created: New York: AMS Press, 1978.
Description: xii, 234 p.: maps; 19 cm.
ISBN: 0404154107
Notes: Reprint of the 1934 ed. published by Methuen, London. Includes index. Bibliography: p. 205-227.
Subjects: Nikopoli, Battle of, 1396. Crusades--Later, 13th, 14th, and 15th centuries.
LC Classification: D172 .A83 1978
Dewey Class No.: 940.1/7

Atiya, Aziz Suryal, 1898-
The crusade: historiography and bibliography.
Published/Created: Bloomington, Indiana University Press, 1962.

Description: 170 p. 21 cm.
Notes: "A companion volume to
Crusade: commerce and culture."
Subjects: Crusades--
Historiography. Crusades--
Bibliography.
LC Classification: Z6207.C97 A8
Dewey Class No.: 016.94018

Atiya, Aziz Suryal, 1898-
The crusade: historiography and
bibliography / Aziz S. Atiya.
Published/Created: Westport,
Conn.: Greenwood Press, 1976,
c1962.
Description: 170 p.; 23 cm.
ISBN: 0837183642
Notes: A companion volume to
Crusade: commerce and culture.
Reprint of the ed. published by
Indiana University Press,
Bloomington. Includes index.
Subjects: Crusades--
Bibliography. Crusades--
Historiography.
LC Classification: Z6207.C97 A8
1976 D157
Dewey Class No.: 016.9401/8

Baldwin, Marshall Whithed, 1903-
Raymond III of Tripolis and the
fall of Jerusalem (1140-1187) /
by Marshall Whithed Baldwin.
Published/Created: New York:
AMS Press, 1978.
Description: viii, 177 p., [1] fold.
leaf of plates: ill.; 23 cm.

ISBN: 0404154115
Notes: Originally presented as the
author's thesis, Princeton
University, 1933. Reprint of the
1936 ed. published by Princeton
University Press, Princeton, N.J.
Includes index. Bibliography: p.
[161]-172.
Subjects: Raymond III, of
Tripolis, 1140 (ca.)-1187.
Crusades--Biography. Jerusalem-
-History--Latin Kingdom, 1099-
1244.
LC Classification: D194.R39 B34
1978
Dewey Class No.: 956.94/03/092

Barber, Malcolm.
Crusaders and heretics, 12th-14th
centuries / Malcolm Barber.
Published/Created: London;
Brookfield, Vt.: Variorum, 1995.
Description: 1 v. (various
pagings): ill.; 23 cm.
ISBN: 0860784762 (alk. paper)
Notes: Includes bibliographical
references and index.
Subjects: Crusades. Heresies,
Christian--History--Middle Ages,
600-1500. Europe--Church
history--600-1500. Europe--
History--476-1492.
Series: Collected studies; CS498.
Variant Series: Collected studies
Series; CS498
LC Classification: BR270 .B37
1995

Dewey Class No.: 270.5 20

Barker, Ernest, Sir, 1874-1960.
  The Crusades.
  Published/Created: Freeport,
  N.Y., Books for Libraries Press
  [1971]
  Description: 112 p. 23 cm.
  ISBN: 0836958233
  Notes: Reprint of the 1923 ed.
  Includes bibliographical
  references.
  Subjects: Crusades.
  LC Classification: D158 .B3
  1971
  Dewey Class No.: 940.1/8

Barrington, Michael.
  Blaye, Roland, Rudel and the
  Lady of Tripoli; a study in the
  relations of poetry to life, A. D.
  731-1950.
  Published/Created: Salisbury
  [Eng.] Bennett Bros., 1953.
  Description: xvi, 242 p. illus.,
  maps, facsims. 26 cm.
  Notes: "Edition limited to three
  hundred copies." Errata slips
  inserted. Bibliographical
  footnotes.
  Subjects: Jaufré Rudel, 12th
  century. Roland (Legendary
  character) Crusades.
  LC Classification: PC3330.J3 B3
  Dewey Class No.: 849.129

Beaufort, Simon.
  Murder in the Holy City / Simon
  Beaufort.
  Edition Information: 1st ed.
  Published/Created: New York:
  St. Martin's Press, 1998.
  Description: 277 p.; 22 cm.
  ISBN: 0312195664
  Subjects: Knights and
  knighthood--Fiction. Crusades--
  Fiction. Jerusalem--Fiction.
  Genre/Form: Detective and
  mystery stories. Historical fiction.
  LC Classification: PR6052.E2226
  M8 1998
  Dewey Class No.: 823/.914 21

Bell, Gerard.
  Crusaders. Illustrated by John
  Lathey.
  Published/Created: New York, St.
  Martin's Press, 1967.
  Description: 64 p. illus., maps,
  plan. 25 cm.
  Notes: Bibliography: p. 62.
  Subjects: Crusades--Juvenile
  literature.
  LC Classification: D158 .B4
  Dewey Class No.: 940.1

Belloc, Hilaire, 1870-1953.
  The crusade, the world's debate,
  by Hilaire Belloc.
  Published/Created: London [etc.]
  Cassell and company, ltd. [1937]
  Description: 7 p.l., 3-314 p. illus.
  (maps) diagrs. 23 cm.

Subjects: Crusades.
LC Classification: D157 .B38

Belloc, Hilaire, 1870-1953.
The crusades; the world's debate,
by Hilaire Belloc.
Published/Created: Milwaukee,
The Bruce publishing company
[c1937]
Description: x, 331 p. illus.
(maps) diagrs. 23 cm.
Subjects: Crusades.
LC Classification: D157 .B38

Ben-Ami, Aharon.
Social change in a hostile
environment; the crusader's
Kingdom of Jerusalem.
Published/Created: Princeton,
N.J., Princeton University Press,
1969.
Description: viii, 193 p. 3 maps.
23 cm.
Notes: Bibliography: p. 189-190.
Subjects: Social history--
Medieval, 500-1500. Social
change. Crusades. Jerusalem--
History--Latin Kingdom, 1099-
1244.
Series: Princeton studies on the
Near East
LC Classification: D182 .B4
Dewey Class No.: 956.9403

Bennetts, Pamela.
Richard and the knights of God /
Pamela Bennetts.

Published/Created: South
Yarmouth, Ma.: J. Curley, 1977,
c1973.
Description: 512 p.; 22 cm.
ISBN: 0893400696
Notes: Large print ed.
Subjects: Richard I, King of
England, 1157-1199 --Fiction.
Crusades--Third, 1189-1192--
Fiction. Large type books.
Genre/Form: Biographical
fiction.
LC Classification: PZ4.B4734
Ri6 PR6052.E533
Dewey Class No.: 823/.9/14

Benvenisti, Meron, 1934-
The crusaders in the Holy Land
[by] Meron Benvenisti.
Edition Information: [1st
American ed.]
Published/Created: New York,
Macmillan [1972, c1970]
Description: xiii, 408 p. illus. 25
cm.
Notes: Includes bibliographical
references.
Subjects: Crusades. Jerusalem--
History--Latin Kingdom, 1099-
1244.
LC Classification: D182 .B44
1972
Dewey Class No.: 915.694/4/033

Benvenisti, Meron, 1934-
The crusaders in the Holy Land
[by] Meron Benvenisti. [English

version: Pamela Fitton]
Published/Created: Jerusalem,
Israel Universities Press [1970]
Description: xiii, 408 p. illus.,
maps (1 fold. inserted), plans. 26
cm.
Notes: Bibliography: p. 393.
Subjects: Crusades. Jerusalem--
History--Latin Kingdom, 1099-
1244.
LC Classification: D182 .B44
Dewey Class No.: 915.694/4/033
Language Code: engheb

Bercovici, Konrad, 1882
The crusades, by Konrad
Bercovici.
Published/Created: New York,
Cosmopolitan book corporation,
1929.
Description: 6 p. l., 3-314, [2] p.
front., plates. 25 cm.
Subjects: Crusades. Templars.
LC Classification: D157 .B4

Berger, Élie, 1850-1925.
Saint Louis et Innocent IV, étude
sur les rapports de la France et du
Saint-Siége.
Published/Created: Paris, Thorin,
1893.
Description: iii, 427 p. 25 cm.
Subjects: Louis IX, King of
France, 1214-1270. Innocentius
IV, Pope, d 1254. Catholic
Church--Relations (diplomatic)
with France. Crusades--Seventh,

1248-1250. France--Foreign
relations--Catholic Church.
LC Classification: BX1240 .B45

Biel, Timothy L.
The crusades / by Timothy Levi
Biel.
Published/Created: San Diego,
CA: Lucent Books, c1995.
Description: 128 p.: ill., maps;
24 cm.
ISBN: 1560062452 (alk. paper):
Notes: Includes bibliographical
references (p. 120-123) and
index.
Subjects: Crusades--Juvenile
literature. Crusades.
Series: World history
Series
LC Classification: D157 .B54
1995
Dewey Class No.: 909.07 20

Billings, Malcolm.
The cross & the crescent: a
history of the Crusades / Malcolm
Billings.
Published/Created: New York:
Sterling Pub. Co., 1988, c1987.
Description: 239, [1] p.: ill.
(some col.); 26 cm.
ISBN: 0806969040
Notes: "Accompanies the BBC
Radio
Series The Cross and the
crescent, first broadcast
beginning in January 1987"--T.p.

verso. Includes index.
Bibliography: p. 239-[240].
Subjects: Crusades.
LC Classification: D157 .B55
1988
Dewey Class No.: 909.07 19

Bloss, C. A. (Celestia Angenette),
1812-1855.
Heroines of the crusades / by
C.A. Bloss.
Published/Created: Muscatine,
Iowa: R.M. Burnett, 1852, c1853.
Description: 496 p., [4] leaves of
plates: ports.; 24 cm.
Notes: Added engraved t.p.,
illustrated. "
Notes": p. [461]-496. LC copy
imperfect: p. 495-496 and 1 port.
wanting.
Subjects: Crusades--Biography.
Women--Biography.
LC Classification: D156 .B6
1853b
Dewey Class No.: 909.07 19

Bloss, Celestia Angenette, 1812-
1855.
Heroines of the crusades.
Published/Created: Detroit, Herr,
Doughty & Lapham, 1853.
Description: xi p., 3 l., [19]-496
p. ports. 24 cm.
Subjects: Crusades. Woman--
Biography.
LC Classification: D156 .B6

Boas, Adrian J., 1952-
Crusader archaeology: the
material culture of the Latin East
/ Adrian J. Boas.
Published/Created: London; New
York: Routledge, 1999.
Description: xxi, 267 p.: ill.,
maps; 24 cm.
ISBN: 0415173612
Notes: Includes bibliographical
references (p. [238]-255) and
index.
Subjects: Crusades. Excavations
(Archaeology)--Jerusalem.
Jerusalem--History--Latin
Kingdom, 1099-1244. Jerusalem-
-Antiquities.
LC Classification: D183 .B63
1999
Dewey Class No.: 956/.014 21

Boase, T. S. R. (Thomas Sherrer
Ross), 1898-1974.
Castles and churches of the
crusading kingdom; by T. S. R.
Boase; with colour photographs
by Richard Cleave.
Published/Created: London, New
York [etc.] Oxford U.P., 1967]
Description: xiv, 121 p. illus., 24
col. plates, maps, plans. 30 cm.
Notes: Bibliography: p. 114.
Subjects: Castles--Latin Orient--
History--To 1500. Church
buildings--Latin Orient--History--
To 1500. Architecture, Medieval-
-Latin Orient. Crusades.

LC Classification: NA1460 .B6
1967
Dewey Class No.: 726/.095694

Boase, T. S. R. (Thomas Sherrer
Ross), 1898-1974.
Kingdoms and strongholds of the
Crusaders [by] T. S. R. Boase.
Published/Created: London,
Thames and Hudson, 1971.
Description: 272 p.; illus. (some
col.), geneal tables, map. 25 cm.
ISBN: 0500250294
Notes: Bibliography: p. 254-257.
Subjects: Crusades.
LC Classification: D157 .B6
Dewey Class No.: 915.6

Bradford, Ernle Dusgate Selby.
The sundered cross; the story of
the Fourth Crusade [by] Ernle
Bradford.
Published/Created: Englewood
Cliffs, N.J., Prentice-Hall [1967]
Description: xiii, 231 p. illus.,
maps (on lining papers), port. 24
cm.
Notes: Bibliography: p. 221-222.
Subjects: Crusades--Fourth,
1202-1204.
LC Classification: D164.A3 B7
Dewey Class No.: 940.1/8

Bradford, Ernle Dusgate Selby.
The sword and the scimitar: the
saga of the Crusades / Ernle
Bradford.

Published/Created: [New York]:
Putnam, 1974.
Description: 239, [1] p.: ill.
(some col.); 26 cm.
ISBN: 0399113754:
Notes: Includes index.
Bibliography: p. [240]
Subjects: Crusades.
LC Classification: D157 .B77
Dewey Class No.: 940.1/8

Bradford, Karleen.
There will be wolves / Karleen
Bradford.
Edition Information: 1st
American ed.
Published/Created: New York:
Lodestar Books, 1996.
Description: 195 p.: map; 22 cm.
ISBN: 0525675396 (alk. paper)
Subjects: Crusades--First, 1096-
1099--Juvenile fiction. Crusades-
-First, 1096-1099--Fiction.
LC Classification: PZ7.B72285
Th 1996
Dewey Class No.: [Fic] 20

Brander, Michael.
The Mark of Gleneil / by Michael
Brander.
Published/Created:
Whittingehame: Gleneil Press,
1998.
Description: viii, 162 p.; 22 cm.
ISBN: 0952533081
Subjects: Crusades--Third, 1189-
1192--Fiction. Scots--Middle

East--Fiction. Clans--Fiction.
Highlands (Scotland)--Fiction.
Middle East--Fiction.
Genre/Form: Historical fiction.
LC Classification:
PR6052.R2764 M3 1998
Dewey Class No.: 823/.914 21

Breakenridge, John, 1820-1854.
The Crusades, and other poems.
Published/Created: Kingston
[Ont.] J. Rowlands, 1846.
Description: viii p., 1 l., [11]-327
p. 25 cm.
Subjects: Bible--History of
Biblical events. Crusades--
Poetry.
LC Classification: PR4161 .B58

Bridge, Antony.
Richard the Lionheart / Antony
Bridge.
Published/Created: New York:
M. Evans, c1989
Description: viii, 259 p., [11] p.
of plates: ill., maps; 24 cm.
ISBN: 0871316242:
Notes: Includes bibliographical
references (p. [251]) and index.
Subjects: Richard I, King of
England, 1157-1199. Crusades--
Third, 1189-1192. Great Britain--
Kings and rulers--Biography.
Great Britain--History--Richard I,
1189-1199.
LC Classification: DA207 .B75
1989

Dewey Class No.: 942.03/2/092
B 20

Bridge, Antony.
The Crusades / Antony Bridge.
Published/Created: New York: F.
Watts, 1982, c1980.
Description: 314 p., [24] leaves
of plates: ill. (some col.); 25 cm.
ISBN: 0531098729
Notes: Includes bibliographical
references and index.
Subjects: Crusades.
LC Classification: D157 .B85
1982
Dewey Class No.: 909.07 19

Brodman, James.
Ransoming captives in crusader
Spain: the Order of Merced on
the Christian-Islamic frontier /
James William Brodman.
Published/Created: Philadelphia:
University of Pennsylvania Press,
1986.
Description: xi, 196 p.: ill; 24
cm.
ISBN: 0812280016
Notes: Includes index.
Bibliography: p. [181]-188.
Subjects: Mercedarians--Spain--
History. Church history--Middle
Ages, 600-1500. Civilization,
Islamic. Crusades. Spain--Church
history.
Series: The Middle Ages
LC Classification: BX3800.Z5

S725 1986
Dewey Class No.: 271/.45/046 19

Brouwer, Sigmund, 1959-
Knights honor / Sigmund
Brouwer.
Published/Created: Nashville: T.
Nelson, c1997.
Description: xviii, 60 p.; 18 cm.
ISBN: 0849940354
Series: Brouwer, Sigmund, 1959-
CyberQuest; #2.
Variant Series: CyberQuest; #2
LC Classification: PZ7.B79984
Kn 1997
Dewey Class No.: [Fic] 21

Brundage, James A.
Medieval canon law and the
crusader, by James A. Brundage.
Published/Created: Madison,
University of Wisconsin Press,
1969. ·
Description: xx, 244 p. front. 24
cm.
ISBN: 0299054802
Notes: Bibliography: p. 199-227.
Subjects: Crusades. Vows (Canon
law) Privileges and immunities,
Ecclesiastical. Law, Medieval.
LC Classification: D160 .B72
Dewey Class No.: 940.1/8

Brundage, James A.
The Crusades, a documentary
survey.
Published/Created: Milwaukee,

Marquette University Press,
1962.
Description: 318 p. illus. 23 cm.
Notes: Translations from original
documentary accounts of the
times woven together with
narrative introductions.
Subjects: Crusades.
LC Classification: D157 .B88
Dewey Class No.: 940.18
Language Code: engund

Brundage, James A.
The Crusades, holy war, and
canon law / James A. Brundage.
Published/Created: Aldershot,
Hampshire, Great Britain:
Variorum; Brookfield, Vt., USA:
Gower, c1991.
Description: 1 v. (various
pagings): 1 ill.; 23 cm.
ISBN: 0860782913
Notes: Includes bibliographical
references and index.
Subjects: Canon law--History.
Crusades. War--Religious
aspects--Catholic Church--
History.
Series: Collected studies; CS338
LC Classification: LAW
Dewey Class No.: 262.9/09 20

Brundage, James A., ed.
The Crusades, motives and
achievements. Edited with an
introd. by James A. Brundage.
Published/Created: Boston, Heath

[1964]
Description: xiv, 89 p. 24 cm.
Notes: Bibliography: p. 88-89.
Subjects: Crusades--Influence.
Series: Problems in European
civilization
LC Classification: D160 .B7
Dewey Class No.: 940.18082

Buehr, Walter.
The crusaders.
Published/Created: New York,
Putnam [1959]
Description: 96 p. illus. 22 cm.
Subjects: Crusades--Juvenile
literature.
LC Classification: D158 .B85
Dewey Class No.: 940.18

Bull, Marcus Graham.
Knightly piety and the lay
response to the First Crusade: the
Limousin and Gascony, c. 970-c.
1130 / Marcus Bull.
Published/Created: Oxford:
Clarendon Press; Oxford; New
York: Oxford University Press,
1993.
Description: xiv, 328 p.: maps;
22 cm.
ISBN: 0198203543 (alk. paper):
Notes: Includes bibliographical
references (p. [289]-313) and
index.
Subjects: Knights and
knighthood--France--History.
Crusades--First, 1096-1099.

Limousin (France)--Religious life
and customs. Gascony (France)--
Religious life and customs.
LC Classification: BR844 .B85
1993
Dewey Class No.:
282/.4466/09021 20

Burns, Robert Ignatius.
Islam under the crusaders,
colonial survival in the thirteenth-
century Kingdom of Valencia
[by] Robert Ignatius Burns.
Published/Created: Princeton,
N.J., Princeton University Press
[1973]
Description: xxxi, 475 p. illus. 25
cm.
ISBN: 0691052077
Notes: Bibliography: p. 421-456.
Subjects: James I, King of
Aragon, 1208-1276. Pedro III,
King of Aragon, 1239-1285.
Imperialism--History--To 1500.
Mudéjares. Civilization, Islamic.
Crusades. Valencia (Spain:
Region)--History.
LC Classification: DP302.V205
B83
Dewey Class No.: 946/.76

Burns, Robert Ignatius.
Medieval colonialism:
postcrusade exploitation of
Islamic Valencia / Robert
Ignatius Burns.
Published/Created: Princeton,

N.J.: Princeton University Press, [1975]
Description: xxiv, 394 p., [4] leaves of plates: ill.; 24 cm.
ISBN: 0691052271
Notes: Includes index.
Bibliography p. 349-375.
Subjects: James I, King of Aragon, 1208-1276. Taxation--Spain--Valencia (Region)--History--To 1500. Mudéjares. Crusades. Valencia (Spain: Region)--Economic conditions.
LC Classification: HC387.V3 B87
Dewey Class No.: 336.2/00946/76

Burns, Robert Ignatius.
Moors and crusaders in Mediterranean Spain / Robert I. Burns.
Published/Created: London: Variorum, 1978.
Description: [318] p.: ill.; 24 cm.
ISBN: 086078018X:
Notes: Includes bibliographical references and index.
Subjects: Civilization, Islamic. Muslims--Spain--History. Crusades. Spain--History--711-1516. Valencia (Spain: Region)--History. Mediterranean Region--History--476-1517.
Variant Series: Variorum reprint: Collected studies [Series]; CS 73
LC Classification: DP99 .B87

Dewey Class No.: 946/.02

Byrne, Donn, 1889-1928.
Crusade / by Donn Byrne.
Published/Created: Boston: Little, Brown and Company, 1928.
Description: 250 p.; 20 cm.
Notes: "Three hundred and sixty-five copies of this limited edition have been printed, and are inscribed by the author ..."
Subjects: Crusades--Sixth, 1228-1229--Fiction.
LC Classification: PZ3.B9963 Cr
Dewey Class No.: 823.91

Cadnum, Michael.
The book of the lion / Michael Cadnum.
Published/Created: New York: Viking, 2000.
Description: 204 p.; 22 cm.
ISBN: 0670883867 (hc)
Subjects: Knights and knighthood--Fiction. Crusades--Third, 1189-1192--Fiction. Middle Ages--Fiction.
LC Classification: PZ7.C1172 Bo 2000
Dewey Class No.: [Fic] 21

Cairns, Trevor.
The Middle Ages.
Published/Created: Minneapolis, Lerner Publications Co. [1975, c1972]
Description: ix, 99 p. illus. (part

col.) 21 x 23 cm.
ISBN: 0822508044 (lib. bdg.)
Notes: "Published in cooperation
with Cambridge University
Press."
Subjects: Civilization, Medieval--
Juvenile literature. Civilization,
Medieval. Middle Ages.
Variant Series: His The
Cambridge introduction to history
LC Classification: CB351 .C23
1975
Dewey Class No.: 914/.03/1

Calin, William.
Crown, cross, and "fleur-de-lis":
an essay on Pierre Le Moyne's
baroque epic "Saint Louis" /
William Calin.
Published/Created: Saratoga,
Calif.: Anma Libri, 1977.
Description: 77 p.; 24 cm.
ISBN: 0915838346
Notes: Includes bibliographical
references.
Subjects: Le Moyne, Pierre,
1602-1671. Saint Lovys. Louis
IX, King of France, 1214-1270 --
In literature. Epic poetry, French-
-History and criticism. Baroque
literature--History and criticism.
Medievalism--France--History--
17th century. Crusades in
literature.
Series: Stanford French and
Italian studies; v. 6
LC Classification: PQ1817.L47

S333
Dewey Class No.: 841/.4

Campbell, G. A. (George Archibald),
1900-
The crusades, by G. A. Campbell.
Published/Created: London,
Duckworth [1935]
Description: 480 p. 2 illus.
(maps) 22 cm.
Notes: "Selected bibliography":
p. 471-473.
Subjects: Crusades.
LC Classification: D157 .C3
Dewey Class No.: 940.18

Cardini, Franco.
Europe and Islam / Franco
Cardini; translated by Caroline
Beamish.
Published/Created: Oxford, UK;
Malden, Mass., USA: Blackwell,
2001. Projected Pub. Date: 0105
Description: p. cm.
ISBN: 063119732X (hardcover:
alk. paper) 0631226370 (pbk.:
alk. paper)
Notes: Includes bibliographical
references and index.
Subjects: Crusades. Civilization,
Islamic. Civilization, Medieval.
Islamic Empire--Relations--
Europe. Europe--Relations--
Islamic Empire. Islamic Empire--
History, Military. Islamic
Empire--History--750-1258.
Europe--History--476-1492.

Series: The making of Europe
LC Classification: DS38.3
.C3713 2001
Dewey Class No.: 909/.09767101
21
Language Code: eng ita

Cartlidge, Cherese.
The Crusades: failed holy wars /
by Cherese Cartlidge.
Published/Created: San Diego,
Calif.: Lucent Books, 2002.
Projected Pub. Date: 0201
Description: p. cm.
ISBN: 1560069996 (hardback:
alk. paper)
Notes: Includes bibliographical
references and index.
Subjects: Crusades
Aggressiveness--Religious
aspects. Religous tolerance--
History--To 1500. Jews--
Persecutions--Europe, Western.
Christianity and other religions.
Religion and civilization. Middle
East--History. Europe--Church
history--600-1500.
Series: History's great defeats
LC Classification: D160 .C37
2002
Dewey Class No.: 909.07 21

Chaikin, L. L., 1943-
Behind the veil / Linda Chaikin.
Published/Created: Thorndike,
ME: Thorndike Press, 1998.
Description: 422 p. (large print);

22 cm.
ISBN: 0786215232 (lg. print: hc:
alk. paper)
Subjects: Crusades--First, 1096-
1099--Fiction. Large type books.
Byzantine Empire--History--
Alexius I Comnenus, 1081-1118
Fiction. Genre/Form: Historical
fiction. Christian fiction.
LC Classification: PS3553.H2427
B44 1998
Dewey Class No.: 813/.54 21

Chaikin, L. L., 1943-
Golden palaces / Linda Chaikin.
Published/Created: Minneapolis:
Bethany House, c1996.
Description: 352 p.: map; 21 cm.
ISBN: 1556618654 (pbk.)
Subjects: Crusades--First, 1096-
1099--Fiction. Genre/Form:
Historical fiction. Christian
fiction.
Series: Chaikin, L. L., 1943-
Royal pavilions; 2.
Variant Series: The royal
pavilions; 2
LC Classification: PS3553.H2427
G65 1996
Dewey Class No.: 813/.54 20

Chaikin, L. L., 1943-
Swords and scimitars / Linda
Chaikin.
Published/Created: Thorndike,
Me.: Thorndike Press, 1997.
Editors: Chaikin, L. L., 1943-

Swords & scimitars.
Description: 445 p. (large print):
map; 23 cm.
ISBN: 0786212365 (lg. print: hc:
alk. paper)
Notes: Rev. ed. of: Swords &
scimitars. c1993.
Subjects: Crusades--First, 1096-
1099--Fiction. Large type books.
Genre/Form: Historical fiction.
Christian fiction.
Series: Thorndike large print
Christian fiction
Series
LC Classification: PS3553.H2427
S9 1997
Dewey Class No.: 813/.54 21

Chazan, Robert.
European Jewry and the First
Crusade / Robert Chazan.
Published/Created: Berkeley:
University of California Press,
c1987.
Description: ix, 380 p.; 22 cm.
ISBN: 0520055667 (alk. paper)
Notes: Includes index.
Bibliography: p. 357-367.
Subjects: Jews--Germany--
History--1096-1147. Jews--
Persecutions--Germany.
Crusades--First, 1096-1099--
Jews--Germany. Germany--
Ethnic relations.
LC Classification: DS135.G31
C45 1987
Dewey Class No.: 943/.004924

19

Chazan, Robert.
God, humanity, and history: the
Hebrew First Crusade narratives /
Robert Chazan.
Published/Created: Berkeley, CA:
University of California Press,
c2000.
Description: xi, 270 p.; 24 cm.
ISBN: 0520221273 (cloth: alk.
paper)
Notes: Includes bibliographical
references (p. 257-262) and
index.
Subjects: Jews--Germany--
History--1096-1147--Sources.
Jews--Persecutions--Germany--
History--Sources. Jewish
martyrs--Germany--Biography--
Sources. Crusades--First, 1096-
1099--Sources. Germany--Ethnic
relations--Sources.
LC Classification: DS135.G31
C53 2000
Dewey Class No.: 943/.004924
21

Chazan, Robert.
In the year 1096: the First
Crusade and the Jews / Robert
Chazan.
Published/Created: Philadelphia:
Jewish Publication Society, 1996.
Description: xv, 186 p.: map; 24
cm.
ISBN: 0827605757

Notes: Includes bibliographical references (p. [171]-177) and index.
Subjects: Jews--Germany--History--1096-1147. Jews--Persecutions--Germany. Crusades--First, 1096-1099. Germany--Ethnic relations.
LC Classification: DS135.G31 C446 1996
Dewey Class No.: 943/.004924 20

Chenevix Trench, Charles Pocklington,
A sword for hire,
Published/Created: London, W. H. Allen [1951]
Description: 248 p. 20 cm.
Notes: Serial.
Subjects: Crusades--First, 1096-1099--Fiction.
LC Classification: PZ4.C518 Sw

Child, John, 1951-
The Crusades / John Child, Nigel Kelly, Martyn Whittock.
Edition Information: 1st Amer. ed.
Published/Created: New York: P. Bedrick, 1996.
Editors: Kelly, Nigel. Whittock, Martyn J.
Description: 64 p.: col. ill., col. maps; 27 cm.
ISBN: 0872261190
Notes: Includes bibliographical references and index.
Subjects: Crusades--Juvenile literature.
Series: Biographical history
LC Classification: D157 .C45 1996
Dewey Class No.: 909.07 20

Choniates, Nicetas, ca. 1140-1213.
O city of Byzantium: annals of Niketas Choniates / translated by Harry J. Magoulias.
Published/Created: Detroit: Wayne State University Press, 1984.
Editors: Magoulias, Harry J.
Description: xxix, 441 p., [4] p. of plates: ill.; 27 cm.
ISBN: 0814317642
Notes: Includes index.
Bibliography: p. 415-418.
Subjects: Crusades--Fourth, 1202-1204. Byzantine Empire--History--Comneni Dynasty, 1081-1185. Byzantine Empire--History--Angeli, 1185-1204.
Series: Byzantine texts in translation
LC Classification: DF606 .C5313 1984
Dewey Class No.: 949.5/02 21
Language Code: enggrc

Christiansen, Eric, 1937-
The northern Crusades / Eric Christiansen.
Edition Information: 2nd, new ed.

Published/Created: London, England; New York, N.Y., USA: Penguin, 1997.
Description: xxv, 287 p.: maps; 20 cm.
ISBN: 0140266534
Notes: Includes bibliographical references (p. 271-278) and index.
Subjects: Crusades. Church history--Middle Ages, 600-1500. Civilization, Medieval. Baltic Sea Region--History.
LC Classification: D173 .C47 1997
Dewey Class No.: 909.07 21

Christiansen, Eric, 1937-
The northern crusades: the Baltic and the Catholic frontier, 1100-1525 / Eric Christiansen.
Published/Created: Minneapolis: University of Minnesota Press, 1980.
Description: xv, 273 p., [4] leaves of plates: ill.; 23 cm.
ISBN: 0816609942:
Notes: Includes index.
Bibliography: p. 254-259.
Subjects: Crusades. Church history--Middle Ages, 600-1500. Baltic Sea region--History.
LC Classification: D173 .C47
Dewey Class No.: 940.1/7

Chronicles of the Crusades: nine crusades and two hundred years of bitter conflict for the Holy Land brought to life through the words of those who were actually there / edited by Elizabeth Hallam.
Edition Information: 1st American ed.
Published/Created: New York: Weidenfeld and Nicolson, c1989.
Editors: Hallam, Elizabeth M.
Description: 400 p.: ill. (some col.), maps; 29 cm.
ISBN: 1555843654:
Notes: Includes bibliographical references (p. 384-386) and index.
Subjects: Crusades--Sources.
LC Classification: D151 .C56 1989
Dewey Class No.: 909.07 20

Chronicles of the crusades; contemporary narratives of the crusade of Richard Coeur de Lion, by Richard of Devizes and Geoffery de Vinsauf; and of the crusade of Saint Louis, by Lord John de Joinville. With illustrative notes and an index.
Published/Created: London, New York, G. Bell & sons, 1892.
Editors: Richard, of Devizes, fl. 1191. Chronicon de rebus gestis Ricardi primi. Ricardus, canonicus Sanctae Trinitatis londoniensis. Itinerarium peregrinorum et gesta regis

Ricardi. Joinville, Jean, sire de, 1224?-1317? Histoire de saint Louis. Giles, J. A. (John Allen), 1808-1884, tr. Johnes, Thomas, 1748-1816, tr.
Description: v, [1], 562 p. col. front. 19 cm.
Subjects: Richard I, King of England, 1157-1199. Louis IX, King of France, 1214-1270 Crusades.
LC Classification: D151 .C55

Church, Alfred John, 1829-1912.
The crusaders, a story of the war for the holy sepulchre, by the Rev. A.J. Church; with illustrations by George Morrow. Published/Created: New York, N.Y., The Macmillan Company, 1905.
Description: vii, 321 p. 8 col. plates 20 cm.
Subjects: Crusades--Fiction.
LC Classification: PZ8.1.C473 Cru

Cipollone, Giulio.
Cristianita--Islam: cattivita e liberazione in nome di Dio: il tempo di Innocenzo III dopo "il 1187" / Giulio Cipollone. Published/Created: Roma: Editrice Pontificia Universita gregoriana, 1992.
Description: xxxiii, 553 p.; 26 cm.

ISBN: 8876526498
Notes: Includes bibliographical references (p. [xvii]-xxxiii) and index.
Subjects: Innocent III, Pope, 1160- or 61-1216. Catholic Church--History. Trinitarians--History. Church history--Middle Ages, 600-1500. Crusades--Third, 1189-1192. Prisoners--Mediterranean Region. Islam--Relations--Christianity. Christianity and other religions--Islam. Mediterranean Region--Church history.
Series: Miscellanea historiae pontificiae; v. 60.
Variant Series: Miscellanea historiae pontificiae; vol. 60
LC Classification: BX1236 .C48 1992
Dewey Class No.: 282/.09/022 20

Clari, Robert de, 12th/13th cent.
The conquest of Constantinople. Translated from the Old French of Robert of Clari by Edgar Holmes McNeal. Published/Created: New York, Octagon Books, 1966 [c1936]
Editors: McNeal, Edgar Holmes, 1874-1955 ed. and tr.
Description: 150 p. 24 cm.
ISBN: 0374955298
Notes: Bibliography: p. [137]-144.
Subjects: Crusades--Fourth,

1202-1204. Istanbul (Turkey)--
History--Siege, 1203-1204.
Series: Records of civilization;
sources and studies, no. 23
LC Classification: D164.A3 R62
1966
Dewey Class No.: 940.18
Language Code: engfro

Cobb, Sylvanus, 1823-1887.
The shadow of the guillotine; a
story of the reign of terror; a
novel [also, Gertrude, the
Amazon; a romance of the first
crusade] By Sylvanus Cobb, jr. ...
With illustrations by Warren B.
Davis.
Published/Created: New York, R.
Bonner's sons, 1894.
Description: 2 p.l., 7-429 p.
plates. 20 cm.
Subjects: Crusades--First, 1096-
1099--Fiction. Women soldiers--
Fiction. France--History--
Revolution, 1789-1799--Fiction.
Series: The choice
Series, no. 115
LC Classification: PZ3.C634 Sh
Copy, Issue: PZ3.C634 Sh2

Coe, Frederick Levi, 1883-
Knight of the cross; a story of the
crusades.
Published/Created: New York,
Sloane [1951]
Description: 245 p. illus. 22 cm.
Subjects: Crusades--Fiction.

LC Classification: PZ7.C656 Kn

Cole, Babette.
Supermoo! / Babette Cole.
Published/Created: London: BBC
Books, 1992.
Description: 1 v. (unpaged): col.
ill.; 21 cm.
ISBN: 0563363665:
Subjects: Cows--Fiction. Heroes-
-Fiction. Environmental
protection--Fiction.
LC Classification: PZ7.C6734 Su
1992b
Dewey Class No.: [E] 20

Cole, Penny J.
The preaching of the crusades to
the Holy Land, 1095-1270 /
Penny J. Cole.
Published/Created: Cambridge,
Mass.: Medieval Academy of
America, 1991.
Description: xiv, 281 p.; 24 cm.
ISBN: 0915651033
Notes: Revision of the author's
thesis (Ph. D.)--University of
Toronto, 1985. Includes
bibliographical references (p.
245-264) and index.
Subjects: Preaching--History--
Middle Ages, 600-1500.
Crusades.
Series: Medieval Academy
books; no. 98
LC Classification: BV4207 .C65
1991

Dewey Class No.: 270.4 20

Constable, Giles.
Monks, hermits, and crusaders in
Medieval Europe / Giles
Constable.
Published/Created: London:
Variorum Reprints, 1988.
Description: 1 v. (various
pagings); 23 cm.
ISBN: 0860782212
Notes: Includes bibliographies
and index.
Subjects: Monasticism and
religious orders--History--Middle
Ages, 600-1500. Crusades.
Series: Variorum reprint; CS273
LC Classification: BX2470 .C62
1988
Dewey Class No.: 271/.0094 19

Coolidge, Olivia E.
Tales of the Crusades [by] Olivia
Coolidge.
Published/Created: Boston,
Houghton Mifflin, 1970.
Editors: Doré, Gustave, 1832-
1883, illus.
Description: ix, 225 p. illus. 22
cm.
Notes: "Art adapted from prints
by Gustave Doré."--Dust jacket.
Subjects: Crusades--Juvenile
fiction. Crusades--Fiction.
Knights and knighthood--Fiction.
LC Classification: PZ7.C778 Tal

Dewey Class No.: [Fic]

Corbishley, Mike.
The medieval world / Mike
Corbishley; illustrated by James
Field.
Edition Information: [1st
American ed.]
Published/Created: New York:
Peter Bedrick Books, c1992.
Description: 64 p.: col. ill., col.
maps; 29 cm.
ISBN: 0872263622
Notes: Includes index.
Subjects: Middle Ages--History--
Juvenile literature.
Series: Timelink
LC Classification: D117 .C66
1992
Dewey Class No.: 909.07 20

Corrick, James A.
Life of a Medieval knight / by
James A. Corrick.
Published/Created: San Diego,
Calif.: Lucent Books, c2001.
Description: 96 p.: ill.; 24 cm.
ISBN: 1560068175 (alk. paper)
Series: The way people live
LC Classification: CR4513 .C67
2001
Dewey Class No.: 940.1 21

Cottin, Madame (Sophie), 1770-1807.
The Saracen; or, Matilda and
Malek Adhel, a crusade romance,
from the French of Madame

Cottin, with an historical introduction, by J. Michaud. Published/Created: New York: Printed and published by Isaac Riley, 1810.
Editors: Michaud, J. Fr. (Joseph Fr.), 1767-1839.
Description: 2 v. 18 cm.
Subjects: Crusades--Fiction.
LC Classification: PZ3.C828 S

Cottin, Marie Risteau, called Sophie, 1770-1807.
Matilda, princess of England. A romance of the crusades, Published/Created: New York, W.S. Gottsberger, 1885.
Editors: Raum, Jennie W., tr.
Description: 2 v. 17 cm.
Subjects: Crusades--Fiction.

Cowdrey, H. E. J. (Herbert Edward John)
Popes, monks, and crusaders / H.E.J. Cowdrey.
Published/Created: London: Hambledon Press, 1984.
Description: 1 v. (various pagings); 25 cm.
ISBN: 0907628346
Notes: Collection of articles originally published between 1966 and 1982. Includes bibliographical references and index.
Subjects: Church history--Middle Ages, 600-1500. Papacy--

History--To 1309. Crusades.
Series: History
Series (Hambledon Press); v. 27.
Variant Series: History
Series; v. 27
LC Classification: BR252 .C68 1984
Dewey Class No.: 270 19

Cowdrey, H. E. J. (Herbert Edward John)
The crusades and Latin monasticism, 11th-12th centuries / H.E.J. Cowdrey.
Published/Created: Aldershot, Hampshire, Great Britain; Brookfield, Vt.: Ashgate, c1999.
Description: 1 v. (various pagings); 24 cm.
ISBN: 0860787958 (alk. paper)
Notes: Includes bibliographical references and index.
Subjects: Crusades--Influence. Monasticism and religious orders--History--Middle Ages, Monasticism and religious orders--History--Middle Ages, 600-1500.
Series: Collected studies; CS662.
Variant Series: Variorum collected studies
Series; CS662
LC Classification: D160 .C68 1999
Dewey Class No.: 270.4 21

Cox, George W.
The crusades,
Published/Created: New York, A.
L. Burt company [c1906]
Editors: Ketcham, Henry.
Description: xvii, 300 p. 19 cm.
Subjects: Crusades.
LC Classification: D158 .C88

Cox, George W. (George William),
1827-1902.
The crusades, by George W. Cox
... With a map.
Published/Created: Boston, Estes
and Lauriat, 1874.
Description: 1 p. l., [vii]-xx, 220
p. front. (fold. map) 16 cm.
Subjects: Crusades.
LC Classification: D158 .C862

Cox, George William, 1827-1902.
The Crusades,
Edition Information: 4th ed.
Published/Created: London,
Longmans, Green, and co., 1877.
Description: xx, 220 p. front.
(fold. map) 16 cm.
Subjects: Crusades.
LC Classification: D158 .C87

Cross cultural convergences in the
Crusader period: essays presented
to Aryeh Grabois on his sixty-
fifth birthday / edited by Michael
Goodich, Sophia Menache &
Sylvia Schein.
Published/Created: New York: P.

Lang, c1995.
Editors: Grabors, Aryeh, 1930-
Goodich, Michael, 1944-
Menache, Sophia. Schein, Sylvia.
Description: xxvii, 334 p.: ill.,
map; 24 cm.
ISBN: 0820423548 (hardcover:
alk. paper)
Notes: Includes bibliographical
references. English, French, and
Italian.
Subjects: Grabors, Aryeh, 1930-
--Bibliography. Crusades. Middle
Ages--History. Multiculturalism.
LC Classification: D159 .C76
1995
Dewey Class No.: 909.07 20
Language Code: engfreita

Crusade and settlement: papers read
at the First Conference of the
Society for the Study of the
Crusades and the Latin East and
presented to R.C. Smail; edited
by Peter W. Edbury.
Published/Created: Cardiff, U.K.:
University College Cardiff Press;
Atlantic Highlands, N.J.:
distributed in USA by
Humanities Press, 1985.
Editors: Smail, R. C. Edbury, P.
W. (Peter W.)
Description: x, 281 p.: ill.; 23
cm.
Notes: Includes bibliographies.
Subjects: Crusades--Congresses.
LC Classification: D160 .S63

1983
Dewey Class No.: 909.07 19

Crusade propaganda and ideology: model sermons for the preaching of the cross / [compiled by] Christoph T. Maier.
Published/Created: Cambridge; New York: Cambridge University Press, 2000.
Editors: Maier, Christoph T.
Description: viii, 280 p.; 24 cm.
ISBN: 0521590612
Notes: Sermons in Latin with English transaltions. Includes bibliographical references and index.
Subjects: Crusades--Propaganda. Crusades--Sermons.
LC Classification: D159 .C77 2000
Dewey Class No.: 909.07 21

Crusader Syria in the thirteenth century: the Rothelin continuation of the History of William of Tyre with part of the Eeracles or Acre text / translated by Janet Shirley.
Published/Created: Aldershot, Hants, England; Brookfield, Vt.: Ashgate, c1999.
Description: 156 p.; 24 cm.
ISBN: 1840146060 (hc.)
Notes: Includes bibliographical references and index.
Subjects: Crusades. Syria--

History--750-1260.
Series: Crusade texts in translation; 5
LC Classification: D172 .C78 1999
Dewey Class No.: 940.1/8 21

Crusaders and Muslims in twelfth-century Syria / edited by Maya Shatzmiller.
Published/Created: Leiden; New York: Brill, 1993.
Editors: Shatzmiller, Maya.
Description: xii, 235 p.; 25 cm.
ISBN: 9004097775 9004098291 (pbk.)
Notes: Includes one contribution in French. Papers presented at a conference held Nov. 1988, University of Western Ontario, London, Ont. Includes bibliographical references (p. [217]-231) and index.
Subjects: Crusades--Congresses. Civilization, Islamic--Congresses. Syria--History--750-1260--Congresses.
Series: The medieval Mediterranean, 0928-5520; v. 1
LC Classification: D159 .C78 1993
Dewey Class No.: 956.91/02 20
Language Code: engfre

Crusades. Volume 1, Pilgrims in arms / a BBC TV Production, in association with A&E Network;

directors/producers, Alan Ereira and David Wallace. Portion of Pilgrims in arms
Published/Created: United States: A&E Home Video, 1995.
Editors: Ereira, Alan, direction, production. Wallace, D. (David), 1937- direction, production. Mudd, Roger, 1928- host. Jones, Terry, host. Copyright Collection (Library of Congress)
Description: 1 videocassette of 1 (VHS): sd., col.; 1/2 in. viewing copy.
Notes: Copyright: no reg. Copyright notice on videocassette jacket: British Broadcasting Corporation; 1995. Art and design copyrighted by A&E Television Networks; 1995
Subjects: Crusades. Christian pilgrims and pilgrimages.
Genre/Form: Documentary-- Television mini
Series.
LC Classification: VAE 5168 (viewing copy)

Crusades. Volume 2, Jerusalem / a BBC TV Production, in association with A&E Network; directors/producers, Alan Ereira and David Wallace. Portion of Jerusalem
Published/Created: United States: A&E Home Video, 1995.
Editors: Ereira, Alan, direction, production. Wallace, D. (David), 1937- direction, production. Mudd, Roger, 1928- host. Jones, Terry, host. Copyright Collection (Library of Congress)
Subjects: Crusades. Christian pilgrims and pilgrimages.
Genre/Form: Documentary-- Television mini
Series.
LC Classification: VAE 5169 (viewing copy)

Crusades. Volume 3, Jihad / a BBC TV Production, in association with A&E Network; directors/producers, Alan Ereira and David Wallace. Portion of Jihad
Published/Created: United States: A&E Home Video, 1995.
Editors: Ereira, Alan, direction, production. Wallace, D. (David), 1937- direction, production. Mudd, Roger, 1928- host. Jones, Terry, host. Copyright Collection (Library of Congress)
Subjects: Crusades--Second, 1147-1149. Christian pilgrims and pilgrimages. Genre/Form: Documentary--Television mini Series.
LC Classification: VAE 5170 (viewing copy)

Crusades. Volume 4, Destruction / a BBC TV Production, in

association with A&E Network; directors/producers, Alan Ereira and David Wallace. Portion of Destruction Published/Created: United States: A&E Home Video, 1995. Editors: Ereira, Alan, direction, production. Wallace, D. (David), 1937- direction, production. Mudd, Roger, 1928- host. Jones, Terry, host. Copyright Collection (Library of Congress) Subjects: Crusades--Third, 1189-1192. Crusades--Fourth, 1202-1204. Christian pilgrims and pilgrimages. Genre/Form: Documentary--Television mini Series. LC Classification: VAE 5171 (viewing copy)

Crusades:
Published/Created: Cambridge, Mass., 1965. Description: 23, 19, 19 p. 28 cm. Subjects: Crusades--Bibliography--Catalogs. Series: Its Widener Library shelflist v. 1] LC Classification: Z6207.C97 H3

Daniel, Norman.
Heroes and Saracens: an interpretation of the chansons de geste / Norman Daniel. Published/Created: Edinburgh: Edinburgh University Press,

c1984. Description: 349 p.; 21 cm. ISBN: 0852244304 Notes: Includes index. Bibliography: p. [320]-327. Subjects: Chansons de geste--History and criticism. French poetry--To 1500--History and criticism. Christianity and other religions in literature. Epic poetry, French--History and criticism. Crusades--Romances--History and criticism. Civilization, Medieval, in literature. Paganism in literature. Muslims in literature. Heroes in literature. Islam in literature. Arabs in literature. LC Classification: PQ205 .D36 1984 Dewey Class No.: 841/.1/09 19

Daniel-Rops, Henri, 1901-1965.
Cathedral and crusade; studies of the medieval church, 1050-1350. Translated by John Warrington. Published/Created: New York, Dutton, 1957. Description: 644 p. illus. 22 cm. Notes: Translation of L'église de la cathédrale et de la croisade. Subjects: Church history--Middle Ages, 600-1500. Crusades. LC Classification: BR270 .D312 1957a Dewey Class No.: 270.3

Language Code: engfre

Dann, Geoff.
    Knight / by Geoff Dann.
    Published/Created: New York:
    A.A. Knopf, 1993. Projected Pub.
    Date: 1111
    Description: p. cm.
    ISBN: 0679838821 (trade)
    0679938826 (lib. bdg.)
    Notes: Includes index.
    Subjects: Knights and
    knighthood--Juvenile literature.
    Civilization, Medieval--Juvenile
    literature. Knights and
    knighthood. Civilization,
    Medieval.
    Variant Series: Eyewitness books
    LC Classification: CR4513 .D36
    1993
    Dewey Class No.: 940.1 20

David, Charles Wendell, 1885-
    Robert Curthose, Duke of
    Normandy.
    Published/Created: New York:
    AMS Press, [1982]
    Description: xiv, 271 p.: map; 23
    cm.
    ISBN: 0404170072
    Notes: Reprint. Originally
    published: Cambridge, Mass.:
    Harvard University Press, 1920.
    (Harvard historical studies; v.
    25) Includes index.
    Subjects: Robert II, Duke of
    Normandy, 1054?-1134.

Nobility--France--Normandy--
    Biography. Crusades--First,
    1096-1099. Great Britain--
    History--Norman period, 1066-
    1154. Normandy (France)--
    History--To 1515.
    Series: Harvard historical studies;
    v. 25.
    LC Classification: DC611.N87
    D3 1982
    Dewey Class No.: 942.02/092/4
    B 19

Davies, D.
    Shiraz, a tale of the crusades.
    Published/Created: Ardmore, I.
    T., Press of T. A. Stones, 1896.
    Description: 48 p. 22 cm.
    Subjects: Crusades--Poetry.
    LC Classification: PS1514 .D27

Davis, Christopher, 1928-
    Belmarch a legend of the First
    Crusade.
    Published/Created: New York,
    Viking Press [1964]
    Description: 211 p. 21 cm.
    Subjects: Crusades--First, 1096-
    1099--Fiction.
    LC Classification: PZ4.D2596 Be

Davis, Edwin John, 1826 or 7-
    The invasion of Egypt in A.D.
    1249 (A.H. 647) by Louis IX. of
    France (St. Louis), and a history
    of the contemporary sultans of
    Egypt; by the Rev. E. J. Davis.

Published/Created: London, Sampson Low, Marston and co., limited [1898]
Description: vi, 152 p. pl., map, plan. 22 cm.
Subjects: Crusades--Seventh, 1248-1250. Egypt--History--Invasion of Saint Louis, 1249.
LC Classification: DT96 .D26

Davis, William Stearns, 1877-1930. "God wills it!" A tale of the first crusade, by William Stearns Davis ... with illustrations by Louis Betts ...
Published/Created: New York, The Macmillan Company; London, Macmillan & Co., ltd., 1901.
Description: xi, 552 p. front., 7 pl. 20 cm.
Subjects: Crusades--First, 1096-1099--Fiction.
LC Classification: PZ3.D30 Go

De Leeuw, Adéle, 1899-
Where valor lies [by] Adéle and Cateau De leeuw. Illustrated by William Plummer.
Edition Information: [1st ed.]
Published/Created: Garden City, N.Y., Doubleday, 1959.
Editors: De Leeuw, Cateau, 1903- joint author.
Description: 186 p. illus. 22 cm.
Subjects: Crusades--Seventh, 1248-1250--Fiction.

Variant Series: Clarion books
LC Classification: PZ7.D38 Wh

Documents on the later Crusades, 1274-1580 / edited and translated by Norman Housley.
Published/Created: New York: St. Martin's Press, 1996.
Editors: Housley, Norman.
Description: xiv, 204 p.: ill., map; 23 cm.
ISBN: 0312161786
Notes: Includes bibliographical references and index. Documents originally in Old French, German, Italian, and Spanish.
Subjects: Crusades--Sources.
Series: Documents in history Series
LC Classification: D172 .D63 1996
Dewey Class No.: 909.07 20

Doherty, Katherine M.
King Richard the Lionhearted and the Crusades in world history / Katherine M. Doherty and Craig A. Doherty.
Published/Created: Berkeley Heights, NJ: Enslow, 2002.
Projected Pub. Date: 0201
Editors: Doherty, Craig A.
Description: p. cm.
ISBN: 0766014592
Notes: Includes bibliographical references and index.
Subjects: Richard I, King of

England, 1157-1199 --Juvenile
literature. Richard I, King of
England, 1157-1199. Crusades--
Juvenile literature. Kings, queens,
rulers, etc. Crusades. Great
Britain--History--Richard I,
1189-1199--Juvenile literature.
Great Britain--Kings and rulers--
Biography--Juvenile literature.
Jerusalem--History--Latin
Kingdom, 1099-1244--Juvenile
literature.
Series: In world history
LC Classification: DA207 .D64
2002
Dewey Class No.: 956/.014 B 21

Donovan, Joseph Patrick, 1911-
Pelagius and the Fifth Crusade /
by Joseph P. Donovan.
Edition Information: 1st AMS ed.
Published/Created: New York:
AMS Press, 1978, c1950.
Description: 124 p.; 23 cm.
ISBN: 0404154166
Notes: Reprint of the ed.
published by University of
Pennsylvania Press, Philadelphia.
Bibliography: p. 117-124.
Subjects: Calvani, Pelagio,
Cardinal, d. 1240. Crusades--
Fifth, 1218-1221. Church history-
-Middle Ages, 600-1500.
LC Classification: D165 .D6
1978
Dewey Class No.: 909.07

Donovan, Joseph Patrick, 1911-
The First Crusade as a
contributing factor in the growth
of secularism.
Published/Created: Washington,
1940.
Description: 66 l. 29 cm.
Subjects: Crusades--First, 1096-
1099. Secularism.
LC Classification: D161.3 .D6

Douglas, Amanda M[innie], 1837-
The heroes of the crusades,
Published/Created: Boston, Lee
and Shepard; New York, C. T.
Dillingham, 1890 [1889]
Description: 2 p.l., 349 p. front.,
50 pl. 19 cm.
Subjects: Crusades.
LC Classification: D158 .D73

Dubois, Pierre, fl. 1300.
The recovery of the Holy Land.
Translated with an introd. and
notes by Walther I. Brandt.
Published/Created: New York,
Columbia University Press, 1956.
Editors: Brandt, Walther
Immanuel, 1893- tr.
Description: xvi, 251 p. 24 cm.
Notes: Bibliography: p. [211]-
239.
Subjects: Crusades.
Series: Records of civilization:
sources and studies, no. 51
LC Classification: D152 .D813
Dewey Class No.: 940.18

Language Code: englat

Duggan, Alfred Leo, 1903-
   Lord Geoffrey's fancy.
   Published/Created: [New York]
   Pantheon Books [1962]
   Description: 254 p. 21 cm.
   Subjects: Crusades--Fiction.
   LC Classification: PZ3.D8789 Lo

Duggan, Alfred Leo, 1903-1964.
   Knight with armour.
   Published/Created: London, New
   English Library, 1973.
   Description: 303 p. 18 cm.
   ISBN: 0450013731
   Subjects: Knights and
   knighthood--Fiction. Middle
   Ages--Fiction. Crusades--Fiction.
   Genre/Form: Historical fiction.
   LC Classification: PZ3.D8789
   Kn8 PR6007.U358
   Dewey Class No.: 823/.9/14

Duggan, Alfred Leo, 1903-1964.
   The story of the Crusades, 1097-
   1291. With drawings by C.
   Walter Hodges.
   Published/Created: New York,
   Pantheon Books [1964, c1963]
   Description: 263 p. illus., ports.,
   maps. 21 cm.
   Notes: Bibliography: p. [7]
   Subjects: Crusades.
   LC Classification: D157 .D83
   1964

Dewey Class No.: 940.18

Duran, Frédérique, 1921-
   In the steps of the crusaders.
   Published/Created: New York,
   Hastings House [1959]
   Description: 126 p. plates (part
   col.) map. 31 cm.
   Notes: i. Pernoud, Régine, 1909-
   Subjects: Crusades. Levant--
   Description and travel--Views.
   LC Classification: D160 .D813

Edbury, P. W. (Peter W.)
   Kingdoms of the Crusaders: from
   Jerusalem to Cyprus / Peter
   Edbury.
   Published/Created: Aldershot,
   Hampshire, England; Brookfield,
   Vt.: Ashgate, 1999.
   Description: 1 v. (various
   pagings); 23 cm.
   ISBN: 0860787923
   Subjects: Crusades--Later, 13th,
   14th, and 15th centuries.
   Jerusalem--History--Latin
   Kingdom, 1099-1244. Cyprus--
   History.
   Series: Collected studies; CS653.
   Variant Series: Variorum
   collected studies
   Series; CS653
   LC Classification: D175 .E33
   1999
   Dewey Class No.: 956/.014 21

Edbury, P. W. (Peter W.)
　　The kingdom of Cyprus and the
　　Crusades, 1191-1374 / Peter W.
　　Edbury.
　　Published/Created: Cambridge
　　[England];　New York:
　　Cambridge University Press,
　　1991.
　　Description: xiv, 241 p.: 2 maps;
　　24 cm.
　　ISBN: 0521268761
　　Notes: Includes bibliographical
　　references (p. [212]-224) and
　　index.
　　Subjects: Crusades. Cyprus--
　　History.
　　LC Classification: DS54.6 .E33
　　1991
　　Dewey Class No.: 956.45 20

Edbury, P. W. (Peter W.)
　　William of Tyre, historian of the
　　Latin East / Peter W. Edbury,
　　John Gordon Rowe.
　　Published/Created: Cambridge
　　[England];　New York:
　　Cambridge University Press,
　　1988.
　　Editors: Rowe, John Gordon.
　　Description: x, 187 p.;　22 cm.
　　ISBN: 0521267668
　　Notes: Includes index.
　　Bibliography: p. 175-180.
　　Subjects: William, of Tyre,
　　Archbishop of Tyre, ca. 1130-ca.
　　1190. Historia rerum in partibus
　　transmarinis gestarum. Godfrey,

of Bouillon, ca.1060-1100.
Crusades--First, 1096-1099--
Historiography. Jerusalem--
History--Latin Kingdom, 1099-
1244 Historiography. Latin
Orient--Historiography.
Series: Cambridge studies in
medieval life and thought;　4th
ser., 8
LC Classification: D152.W553
E33 1988
Dewey Class No.: 940.1/8 19

Edgar, John G. (John George), 1834-
1864.
　　The crusades and the crusaders.
　　By John G. Edgar...With eight
　　illustrations by Julian Portch.
　　Published/Created: Boston,
　　Ticknor and Fields, 1860.
　　Description: vii, 1 l., 380 p.
　　front., plates. 18 cm.
　　Notes: "Author's edition."
　　Subjects: Crusades.
　　LC Classification: D157 .E3

Eickhoff, Ekkehard.
　　Friedrich Barbarossa im Orient:
　　Kreuzzug und Tod Friedrichs I. /
　　Ekkehard Eickhoff.
　　Published/Created: Tьbingen: E.
　　Wasmuth, c1977.
　　Description: 199 p., [12] leaves
　　of plates: ill., fold. col. maps;　26
　　cm.
　　ISBN: 3803017165
　　Notes: Includes bibliographical

references.
Subjects: Frederick I, Holy
Roman Emperor, ca. 1123-1190.
Crusades--Third, 1189-1192.
Series: Istanbuler Mitteilungen.
Beiheft; 17
LC Classification: D163.5.G4
E38

Eisner, Michael Alexander.
The crusader: a novel / Michael
Alexander Eisner.
Edition Information: 1st ed.
Published/Created: New York:
Doubleday, 2001. Projected Pub.
Date: 0110
Description: p. cm.
ISBN: 0385502818
Subjects: Crusades--Eighth,
1270--Fiction. Knights and
knighthood--Fiction. Exorcism--
Fiction. Monks--Fiction. Spain--
History--Arab period, 711-1492--
Fiction. Genre/Form: Historical
fiction.
LC Classification: PS3605.I86
C78 2001
Dewey Class No.: 813/.6 21

Eleanor of Aquitaine and the crusade
of the kings: a medieval journey
of discovery travelogue / edited
by Richard Scheuerman and
Arthur Ellis; illustrated by James
LeGette.
Published/Created: Madison, WI:
DEMCO, 2000. Projected Pub.

Date: 1111
Editors: Scheuerman, Richard D.
Ellis, Arthur K.
Description: p. cm.
ISBN: 1885360193
Notes: Includes bibliographical
references and index.
Subjects: Eleanor, of Aquitaine,
Queen, consort of Henry II, King
of England, 1122?-1204. Richard
I, King of England, 1157-1199.
Frederick I, Holy Roman
Emperor, ca. 1123-1190.
Crusades--Third, 1189-1192.
Great Britain--History--Richard I,
1189-1199.
LC Classification: DA209.E6
E42 2000
Dewey Class No.: 909/.1 21

Erdmann, Carl, 1898-1945.
The origin of the idea of crusade /
Carl Erdmann; translated from
the German by Marshall W.
Baldwin and Walter Goffart;
foreword and additional notes by
Marshall W. Baldwin.
Published/Created: Princeton,
N.J.: Princeton University Press,
1977.
Description: xxxvi, 446 p.; 23
cm.
ISBN: 0691052514:
Notes: Translation of Die
Entstehung des
Kreuzzugsgedankens. Includes
index. Bibliography: p. 373-427.

Subjects: Crusades.
LC Classification: D157 .E713
Dewey Class No.: 909.07
Language Code: engger

Europe at the time of the Crusades /
    Rand McNally.
    Published/Created: [Chicago?]:
    Rand McNally & Co., [1992]
    Description: 1 map: col., plastic;
    72 x 105 cm., on sheet 99 x 112
    cm. Scale Information: Scale
    [1:5,100,000]. 51 km. to the cm.
    80 miles to the in. (W 15°--E
    50°/N 57°--N 12°).
    Notes: History wall map with
    "Markable surface." Relief shown
    by hachures. Includes Notes.
    Insets: Mohammedan power
    about 950 -- Asia Minor and
    Syria about 1140 -- Saladin's
    Empire after 1204 together with
    the results of the Fourth Crusade.
    At lower left: 00-998765432. At
    lower right: 20424. Within map
    border: A-450024-29H-1Y-1R-
    1S-1D-2K. LC copy is proof
    sheet.
    Subjects: Crusades--Maps.
    Europe--History--476-1492--
    Maps. Islamic Empire--History--
    750-1258--Maps.
    LC Classification: G5701.S3
    1992

European explorers discover a new
    world (Filmstrip)

Published/Created: Yale
University Press Film Service,
1953.
Editors: Yale University. Press.
Film Service.
Description: 40 fr., b&w, 35 mm.
Notes: With teacher's guide, by
William H. Hartley. Correlated
with The pageant of America,
edited by R. H. Gabriel.
CREDITS: Editor, Clyde M. Hill;
associate editors, Ralph H.
Gabriel, William H. Hartley, May
Hall James.
Subjects: Discoveries (in
geography) America--Discovery
and exploration.
Series: The pageant of America
filmstrips, no. 2 The pageant of
America filmstrips, no. 2.

Finucane, Ronald C.
    Soldiers of the faith: Crusaders
    and Moslems at war / Ronald C.
    Finucane.
    Edition Information: 1st U.S. ed.
    Published/Created: New York:
    St. Martin's Press, c1983.
    Description: 247 p.: ill.; 25 cm.
    ISBN: 0312742568:
    Notes: Includes index.
    Bibliography: p. 242-243.
    Subjects: Crusades.
    LC Classification: D157 .F56
    1983
    Dewey Class No.: 909/.07 19

Forey, Alan, 1933-
    Military orders and crusades /
    Alan Forey.
    Published/Created: Aldershot,
    Hampshire; Brookfield, Vt.:
    Variorum, 1994.
    Description: 1 v. (various
    pagings); 23 cm.
    ISBN: 0860783987 (alk. paper)
    Notes: Includes bibliographical
    references and index.
    Subjects: Military religious
    orders--History. Crusades.
    Series: Collected studies; CS432.
    Variant Series: Collected studies
    Series; CS432
    LC Classification: CR4705 .F67
    1994
    Dewey Class No.: 271/.791 21

Foss, Michael.
    People of the First Crusade /
    Michael Foss.
    Edition Information: 1st U.S. ed.
    Published/Created: New York:
    Arcade Pub.: Distributed by
    Little, Brown and Co., c1997.
    Description: 232 p.: ill., maps;
    25 cm.
    ISBN: 1559704144
    Notes: Includes index.
    Subjects: Crusades--First, 1096-
    1099. Civilization, Medieval.
    LC Classification: D161.2 .F67
    1997
    Dewey Class No.: 940.1/8 21

Foucher de Chartres, 1058?-ca. 1127.
    A history of the expedition to
    Jerusalem, 1095-1127 [by]
    Fulcher of Chartres. Translated
    by Frances Rita Ryan. Edited
    with an introd. by Harold S. Fink.
    Published/Created: New York,
    W. W. Norton [1972, c1969]
    Description: xiv, 348 p. 21 cm.
    ISBN: 0393006700
    Notes: Translation of Historia
    Hierosolymitana. Bibliography:
    p. 305-320.
    Subjects: Crusades--First, 1096-
    1099--Sources.
    LC Classification: D161.1 .F6913
    1972
    Dewey Class No.: 909.07
    Language Code: engund

Foucher de Chartres, 1058?-ca. 1127.
    Chronicle of the First Crusade =
    Fulcheri Carnotensis Historia
    Hierosolymitana / Fulcher of
    Chartres; translated by Martha
    Evelyn McGinty.
    Edition Information: 1st AMS ed.
    Published/Created: New York:
    AMS Press, 1978.
    Description: x, 90 p.: maps; 23
    cm.
    ISBN: 0404154174
    Notes: Reprint of the ed.
    published by the University of
    Pennsylvania Press, Philadelphia,
    which was issued as 3d ser., v. 1
    of Translations and reprints from

the original sources of history.
Includes index. Bibliography: 83-85
Subjects: Crusades--First, 1096-1099--Sources.
Series: Pennsylvania. University. Dept. of History. Translations and reprints from the original sources of history; ser. 3, v. 1.
LC Classification: D161.1 .F6913 1978
Dewey Class No.: 909.07
Language Code: englat

France, John.
Victory in the East: a military history of the First Crusade / John France.
Published/Created: Cambridge [England]; New York, NY, USA: Cambridge University Press, 1994.
Description: xv, 425 p.: maps; 24 cm.
ISBN: 0521419697 (hardback)
Notes: Includes bibliographical references (p. 383-407) and index.
Subjects: Crusades--First, 1096-1099 Military art and science--History--Medieval, 500-1500.
LC Classification: D161.2 .F73 1994
Dewey Class No.: 940.1/8 20

France, John.
Western warfare in the age of the Crusades, 1000-1300 / John France.
Published/Created: Ithaca, N.Y.: Cornell University Press, 1999.
Description: xv, 327 p.: ill., maps; 24 cm.
ISBN: 0801486076 (pbk.: alk. paper) 0801436710 (alk. paper)
Notes: Includes bibliographical references (p. 295-320) and index.
Subjects: Crusades. Military history, Medieval. Military art and science--History.
LC Classification: D160 .F73 1999
Dewey Class No.: 940.1/8 21

Fuller, Thomas, 1608-1661.
The history of the holy war, by Thomas Fuller.
Published/Created: London, W. Pickering, 1840.
Description: xii, 328 p. tables 18 cm.
Notes: Includes bibliographical footnotes.
Subjects: Crusades.
LC Classification: D158 .F96

Gabrieli, Francesco, 1904- comp.
Arab historians of the Crusades; selected and translated from the Arabic sources, by Francesco Gabrieli; translated from the Italian by E. J. Costello.
Published/Created: London,

Routledge & K. Paul, 1969.
Description: xxxvi, 362 p. 23 cm.
ISBN: 0710028741
Notes: Originally published as
Storici arabi delle Crociate.
Torino (Turin), G. Einaudi, 1957.
Bibliography: p. [xxiv]-xxv.
Subjects: Crusades. Crusades--
Sources. Historians, Arab.
Series: The Islamic world
Series
LC Classification: D151 .G313
1969b
Dewey Class No.: 909.07
Language Code: engitaara

Gibb, Christopher.
Richard the Lionheart and the
Crusades / Christopher Gibb;
illustrations by Gerry Wood.
Published/Created: New York:
Bookwright Press, 1985.
Editors: Wood, Gerald, ill.
Description: 60 p.: ill. (some
col.); 24 cm.
ISBN: 0531180115 (lib. bdg.)
Notes: Includes index.
Bibliography: p. 58.
Subjects: Richard I, King of
England, 1157-1199 --Juvenile
literature. Richard I, King of
England, 1157-1199. Crusades--
Third, 1189-1192--Juvenile
literature. Kings, Queens, rulers,
etc. Crusades. Great Britain--
History--Richard I, 1189-1199--
Juvenile literature. Great Britain--

Kings and rulers--Biography--
Juvenile literature.
Series: Life and times
LC Classification: DA207 .G44
1985
Dewey Class No.: 941.03/2/0924
B 92 19

Gibb, H. A. R. (Hamilton Alexander
Rosskeen), Sir, 1895-1971.
The life of Saladin: from the
works of `Imad ad-Din and Baha'
ad-Din, by Sir Hamilton Gibb.
Published/Created: Oxford,
Clarendon Press, 1973.
Editors: Katib al-Isfahani, `Imad
al-Din Muhammad ibn
Muhammad, 1125-1201. Barq al-
Shami. Ibn Shaddad, Baha' al-Din
Yusuf ibn Rafi`, 1145-1234 or 5.
Nawadir al-sultaniyah wa-al-
mahasin al-Yusufiyah.
Description: [5], 76 p. 23 cm.
ISBN: 0198214995
Notes: "Based on a chapter
contributed by the author to the
History of the crusades (ed., K.
Setton), first published by the
University of Pennsylvania Press
(2nd edn., 1969)...." Includes
bibliographical references.
Subjects: Saladin, Sultan of
Egypt and Syria, 1137-1193.
Crusades. Egypt--Kings and
rulers--Biography. Syria--Kings
and rulers--Biography.
LC Classification: DS38.4.S2

G52 1973
Dewey Class No.: 956/.01/0924
B

Gibson, Michael, 1936-
The knights / [author, Michael Gibson].
Published/Created: New York: Arnc Pub., c1979.
Description: 61 p.: col. ill.; 29 cm.
ISBN: 0668047852:
Notes: Includes index.
Subjects: Knights and knighthood--Juvenile literature. Military art and science--History--Medieval, 500-1500 Juvenile literature. Crusades--Juvenile literature. Knights and knighthood. Crusades.
Variant Series: The Living past
LC Classification: CR4513 .G5
Dewey Class No.: 929.7/1/09

Gillingham, John.
Richard I / John Gillingham.
Published/Created: New Haven: Yale University Press, c1999.
Description: xiv, 378 p.: ill., maps; 24 cm.
ISBN: 0300079125 (alk. paper)
Notes: Includes bibliographical references (p. 352-365) and index.
Subjects: Richard I, King of England, 1157-1199. Crusades--Third, 1189-1192. Great Britain--History--Richard I, 1189-1199. Great Britain--Kings and rulers--Biography.
Series: Yale English monarchs
LC Classification: DA207 .G473 1999
Dewey Class No.: 942.03/2/092
B 21

Glass, Dorothy F.
Portals, pilgrimage, and crusade in western Tuscany / Dorothy F. Glass.
Published/Created: Princeton, N.J.: Princeton University Press, c1997.
Description: xvii, 145 p.: ill., maps; 25 cm.
ISBN: 0691011729 (cloth: alk. paper)
Notes: Includes bibliographical references (p. 109-137) and index.
Subjects: Relief (Sculpture), Italian--Italy--Tuscany. Relief (Sculpture), Medieval--Italy--Tuscany. Christian art and symbolism--Medieval, 500-1500--Italy Tuscany. Lintels--Italy--Tuscany. Crusades.
LC Classification: NB1282 .G58 1997
Dewey Class No.: 730/.945/509021 20

Glubb, John Bagot, Sir, 1897-
The lost centuries: from the

Muslim empires to the Renaissance of Europe, 1145-1453 [by] Lieutenant-General Sir John Glubb.
Published/Created: London, Hodder & Stoughton, 1967.
Description: 511 p. maps, plans, tables, diagrs. 23 cm.
ISBN: 0340025956
Notes: Bibliography: p. [493]-498.
Subjects: Crusades. Islamic Empire--History.
LC Classification: DS236 .G58
Dewey Class No.: 909.07

Godfrey, John.
1204, the unholy Crusade / John Godfrey.
Published/Created: Oxford; New York: Oxford University Press, 1980.
Description: xi, 184 p., [8] leaves of plates: ill.; 24 cm.
ISBN: 0192158341:
Notes: Includes index. Bibliography: p. [176]-177.
Subjects: Crusades--Fourth, 1202-1204.
LC Classification: D164 .G6
Dewey Class No.: 949.61/8013 21

Gordon, Alan (Alan R.)
A death in the Venetian quarter: a medieval mystery / Alan Gordon.
Edition Information: 1st ed.

Published/Created: New York: St. Martin's Minotaur, 2002.
Projected Pub. Date: 0203
Description: p. cm.
ISBN: 0312242670
Subjects: Crusades--Fourth, 1202-1204--Fiction. Fools and jesters--Fiction. Istanbul (Turkey)--History--Siege, 1203-1204--Fiction. Genre/Form: Historical fiction. Mystery fiction.
LC Classification: PS3557.O649 D43 2002
Dewey Class No.: 813/.54 21

Gordon, Alan (Alan R.)
Jester leaps in: a medieval mystery / Alan Gordon.
Edition Information: 1st ed.
Published/Created: New York: St. Martin's Minotaur, 2000.
Description: 276 p.; 22 cm.
ISBN: 0312241178
Subjects: Fools and jesters--Fiction. Middle Ages--Fiction. Crusades--Fiction. Genre/Form: Detective and mystery stories. Historical fiction. Spy stories.
LC Classification: PS3557.O649 J47 2000
Dewey Class No.: 813/.54 21

Gray, George Zabriskie, 1838-1889.
The children's crusade;
Published/Created: Boston and New York, Houghton, Mifflin &

company, 1898.
Description: xv, 242 p. front. 19
cm.
Subjects: Crusades. Children's
crusade, 1212.
LC Classification: D169 .G79

Grousset, René, 1885-1952.
The epic of the Crusades.
Translated from the French by
Noл Lindsay.
Published/Created: New York,
Orion Press, 1970.
Description: vi, 280 p. illus. 24
cm.
Notes: Translation of L'épopée
des croisades. Bibliography: p.
[268]-271.
Subjects: Crusades. Jerusalem--
History--Latin Kingdom, 1099-
1244.
LC Classification: D157 .G6713
1970
Dewey Class No.: 909.07
Language Code: engfre

Guibert, Abbot of Nogent-sous-
Coucy, 1053-ca. 1124.
The deeds of God through the
Franks: a translation of Guibert
de Nogent's Gesta Dei per
Francos / [translated and edited
by] Robert Levine.
Published/Created: Woodbridge,
Suffolk, UK; Rochester, NY,
USA: Boydell Press, 1997.
Editors: Levine, Robert, 1933-

Description: 166 p.; 25 cm.
ISBN: 0851156932 (acid-free
paper)
Notes: Includes bibliographical
references (p. 18-19).
Subjects: Crusades--First, 1096-
1099.
LC Classification: D161.1.G83
G47 1997
Dewey Class No.: 909.07 21
Language Code: eng lat
Guilelmus, Abp. of Tyre, ca. 1130-ca.
1190.
Godeffroy of Boloyne; or, The
siege and conqueste of Jerusalem,
by William, Archbishop of Tyre.
Translated from the French by
William Caxton, and printed by
him in 1481. Edited from the
copy in the British Museum, with
introduction,
Notes, vocabulary, and indexes,
by Mary Noyes Colvin, PH. D.
Published/Created: London, Pub.
for the Early English Text
Society by K. Paul, Trench,
Trьbner & Co., 1893.
Editors: Caxton, William, ca.
1422-1491, tr. Colvin, Mary
Noyes, ed.
Description: xli, 348 p. 23 cm.
Notes: Taken from a French
translation of the Historia rerum
in partibus transmarinis gestarum.
Subjects: Godfrey, of Bouillon,
ca. 1060-1100. Crusades--First,
1096-1099.

Variant Series: Early English
Text Society. Extra
Series. No. LXIV
LC Classification: PR1119 .E5
no. 64
Language Code: eng fre

Hagopian, Hovhan.
The relations of the Armenians
and the Franks during the reign of
Leon II, 1186-1219,
Published/Created: [Boston?]
1905.
Description: 39 p. geneal. tab. 26
cm.
Subjects: Armenia--History.
Crusades.
LC Classification: DS186 .H2

Hamilton, Bernard, 1932-
Crusaders, Cathars, and the holy
places / Bernard Hamilton.
Published/Created: Aldershot,
[England]; Brookfield, Vt.:
Ashgate, c1999.
Description: 1 v. (unpaged): ill.;
23 cm.
ISBN: 0860787850 (hb: alk.
paper)
Notes: Includes bibliographical
references and index.
Subjects: Church history--Middle
Ages, 600-1500. Crusades.
Albigenses. Christian shrines.
Latin Orient--Church history.
Series: Collected studies; CS656.
Variant Series: Variorum

collected studies
Series; CS656
LC Classification: BR270 .H36
1999
Dewey Class No.: 270.4 21

Hamilton, Bernard, 1932-
Monastic reform, Catharism, and
the Crusades, (900-1300) /
Bernard Hamilton.
Published/Created: London:
Variorum Reprints, 1979.
Description: [376] p.: ill.; 23 cm.
ISBN: 0860780422:
Notes: Includes one paper in
French. Includes bibliographical
references and index.
Subjects: Monasticism and
religious orders--Europe--
History--Middle Ages, 600-1500.
Heresies, Christian--France--
Languedoc--History--Middle
Ages, 600-1500. Albigenses.
Crusades.
Variant Series: Collected studies;
CS97
LC Classification: BX2590 .H35
Dewey Class No.: 271/.0094 19
Language Code: engfre

Hamilton, Franklin.
The crusades / by Franklin
Hamilton; illustrated by Judith
Ann Lawrence.
Published/Created: [New York]:
The Dial Press, 1965.
Editors: Lawrence, Judith Ann.

Description: 320 p.: ill.; 22 cm.
Notes: Includes index.
Bibliography: p. 307-308.
Subjects: Crusades--Juvenile
literature.
LC Classification: D158 .H33

Hatt, Christine.
The Crusades / Christine Hatt.
Published/Created: New York:
Franklin Watts, 2001. Projected
Pub. Date: 0109
Description: p. cm.
ISBN: 0531146103
Notes: Originally published:
London: Evans Bros., 1999, in
Series: History in writing.
Subjects: Crusades--Juvenile
literature. Crusades.
Series: Documenting history
LC Classification: D157 .H38
2001
Dewey Class No.: 909.07 21

Hauck, Phillip, 1920-
Plum full of prunes / written by
Philip Eugene Hauck; illustrated
by Audrey Rawlings Arena.
Edition Information: 1st ed.
Published/Created: Fresno, CA:
Dab Pub. Co., 1999.
Editors: Arena, Audrey Rawlings,
1950- ill.
Description: [iv], 26 p.: col. ill.;
29 cm.
ISBN: 0966222857
Notes: Includes bibliographical

references (p. [ii]).
Subjects: Prune--Fiction. Plum--
Fiction. Trees--Fiction.
LC Classification: PZ7.H2855 Pl
1999
Dewey Class No.: [Fic] 21

Heath, Ian.
A wargamers' guide to the
Crusades / Ian Heath.
Published/Created: Cambridge,
Eng.: P. Stephens, 1980.
Description: 160 p.: ill.; 24 cm.
ISBN: 0850594308:
Notes: Bibliography: p. 159-160.
Subjects: Crusades. Military art
and science--History--Medieval,
500-1500.
LC Classification: D157 .H4
Dewey Class No.: 909.07 19

Heddaeus, John, 1847-
Lord Ively; an epic poem in xiv
books, by John Heddaeus ...
Published/Created: New York, J.
B. Alden, 1890.
Description: 162 p. 16 cm.
Subjects: Crusades--Third, 1189-
1192--Poetry.
LC Classification: PS1919 .H27

Henty, G. A. (George Alfred), 1832-
1902.
A knight of the White Cross: a
tale of the siege of Rhodes / 2ith
12 illustrations by Ralph
Peacock.

Published/Created: London:
Blackie, 1896.
Editors: Peacock, Ralph, ill.
Description: 392 p.: ill.; 20 cm.
Subjects: Crusades--Later, 13th,
14th, and 15th centuries--Juvenile
fiction. Knights and knighthood--
Juvenile fiction. Crusades--
Fiction. Knights and knighthood-
-Fiction. Rhodes (Greece)--
History--Siege, 1480--Juvenile
fiction. Rhodes (Greece)--Fiction.
LC Classification: PZ7.H4 Kn3
Dewey Class No.: [Fic] 21

Henty, George Alfred, 1832-1902.
Winning his spurs: a tale of the
crusades.
Published/Created: London, S.
Low, Marston, Searle, &
Rivington, limited, 1888.
Description: vii, 324 p. illus. 18
cm.
Subjects: Crusades--Third, 1189-
1192--Fiction.
LC Classification: PZ9.H47 Wi
Microfilm 76650 P
Hewes, Agnes Danforth.
A boy of the lost crusade, by
Agnes Danforth Hewes; with
illustrations by Gustaf Tenggren.
Published/Created: Boston, New
York, Houghton Mifflin
Company, 1923.
Description: 4 p. l., 279 p. col.
front., col. plates. 21 cm.
Notes: Map on lining-papers.

Subjects: Children's Crusade,
1212--Fiction. Childrens crusade,
1212--Fiction. Crusades.
LC Classification: PZ7.H448 Bo

Higgins, Charles J., 1871-
The maid of Kerak.
Published/Created: Boston,
Meador Pub. Co. [1954]
Description: 753 p. illus. 21 cm.
Subjects: Crusades--Fiction.
LC Classification: PZ4.H636 Mai

Hill, John Hugh.
Raymond IV, count of Toulouse
[by] John Hugh Hill [and] Laurita
Lyttleton Hill.
Published/Created: [Syracuse,
N.Y.] Syracuse University Press,
1962.
Editors: Hill, Laurita Lyttleton,
joint author.
Description: 177 p. illus. 22 cm.
Notes: Includes bibliography.
Subjects: Raymond IV, de Saint-
Gilles, Count of Toulouse, d.
1105. Crusades--First, 1096-
1099.
LC Classification: D161.2 .H5
Dewey Class No.: 923.244

Hillenbrand, Carole.
The Crusades: Islamic
perspectives / Carole
Hillenbrand.
Published/Created: New York:
Routledge, 2000.

Description: lvi, 648 p., [16] p. of plates: ill. (some col.), maps (some col.); 25 cm.
ISBN: 0415929148 (pbk.)
Notes: Includes bibliographical references (p. 617-633) and index.
Subjects: Crusades. Islamic Empire--History--750-1258.
LC Classification: DS38.6 .H55 2000
Dewey Class No.: 909/.097671 21

Hills, Ken.
Crusades / by Ken Hills; illustrated by Francis Phillipps.
Edition Information: Library ed.
Published/Created: New York: Marshall Cavendish, 1991.
Editors: Phillipps, Francis, ill.
Description: 32 p.: col. ill., col. maps; 21 cm.
ISBN: 1854352601
Notes: Includes index.
Subjects: Crusades--Juvenile literature. Crusades.
Series: Wars that changed the world
LC Classification: D157 .H55 1991

Hoban, Russell.
Pilgermann / Russell Hoban.
Published/Created: London: J. Cape, 1983.
Description: 240 p.: ill.; 23 cm.

ISBN: 0224020722:
Notes: Includes bibliographical references.
Subjects: Jews--Europe--Fiction. Crusades--First, 1096-1099--Fiction. Genre/Form: Historical fiction. Ghost stories.
LC Classification: PS3558.O336 P5x 1983b   .

Housley, Norman.
Crusading and warfare in medieval and renaissance Europe / Norman J. Housley.
Published/Created: Aldershot, Hampshire: Burlington, Vt.: Ashgate, 2001. Projected Pub. Date: 0106
Description: p. cm.
ISBN: 0860788431
Notes: Collection of essays, articles, etc. originally published 1980-1999. Includes bibliographical references and index. Includes one contribution in French and one in Italian.
Subjects: Crusades. Heresies, Christian--History--Middle Ages, 600-1500. Military religious orders--History. Military art and science--Europe--History--Medieval, 500-1500. Crusades--Later, 13th, 14th, and 15th centuries. Europe--History--476-1492. Europe--History, Military. Europe--Church history--600-1500.

Series: Collected studies; CS712.
Variant Series: Variorum
collected studies
Series; CS712
LC Classification: D157 .H68
2001
Dewey Class No.: 940.1/7 21
Language Code: engfreita

Housley, Norman.
The Italian crusades: the Papal-
Angevin alliance and the
crusades against Christian lay
powers, 1254-1343 / Norman
Housley.
Published/Created: Oxford:
Clarendon Press; New York:
Oxford University Press, 1982.
Description: 293 p.; 22 cm.
ISBN: 0198219253:
Notes: Includes index.
Bibliography: p. [260]-279.
Subjects: Anjou, House of.
Crusades--Later, 13th, 14th, and
15th centuries. Papacy--History--
1309-1378. Papacy--History--To
1309. Naples (Kingdom)--
History--1016-1268. Naples
(Kingdom)--History--Anjou
dynasty, 1268-1442. Sicily
(Italy)--History--1194-1282.
Sicily (Italy)--History--1282-
1409.
LC Classification: DG847.15
.H68 1982
Dewey Class No.: 945/.7 19

Housley, Norman.
The later crusades, 1274-1580:
from Lyons to Alcazar / Norman
Housley.
Published/Created: New York:
Oxford University Press, 1992.
Description: viii, 14, 528 p.: 14
maps; 24 cm.
ISBN: 0198221371 0198221363
(pbk.)
Notes: Includes bibliographical
references (p. [462]-500) and
index.
Subjects: Crusades. Europe--
History--476-1492. Europe--
History--1492-1648.
LC Classification: D202 .H68
1992
Dewey Class No.: 940.1 20

Howe, Norma.
Blue Avenger cracks the code /
Norma Howe.
Edition Information: 1st ed.
Published/Created: New York:
Holt, 2000.
Description: 296 p.; 22 cm.
ISBN: 0805063722 (hc: alk.
paper)
Subjects: Shakespeare, William,
1564-1616 --Authorship--
Juvenile fiction. Shakespeare,
William, 1564-1616 --
Authorship--Fiction. High
schools--Fiction. Schools--
Fiction. Venice (Italy)--Fiction.
Italy--Fiction.

LC Classification: PZ7.H8376
Gq 2000
Dewey Class No.: [Fic] 21

Hubbard, Margaret Ann, 1909-
St. Louis and the Last Crusade.
Illustrated by Harry Barton.
Published/Created: New York,
Vision Books [1958]
Description: 190 p. illus. 22 cm.
Subjects: Louis IX, King of
France, 1214-1270 --Fiction.
Crusades--Fiction.
Variant Series: Vision books, 33
LC Classification: DC91 .H77

Hubbard, Margaret Ann, 1909-
The blue gonfalon. Illustrated by
Shane Miller.
Edition Information: 1st edition.
Published/Created: Garden City,
N.Y., Doubleday, 1960.
Description: 187 p. illus. 22 cm.
Subjects: Crusades--First, 1096-
1099--Fiction.
Variant Series: Clarion books.
LC Classification: PZ7.H859 Bl

Hurley, Frank X., 1940-
The crusader / by Frank X.
Hurley, Jr.
Published/Created: Philadelphia:
Dorrance, [1975] c1974.
Description: 102 p.; 22 cm.
ISBN: 0805920870:
Subjects: Crusades--First, 1096-
1099--Fiction. Genre/Form:

Historical fiction.
LC Classification: PZ4.H964 Cr3
PS3558.U53
Dewey Class No.: 813/.5/4

Ibn al-Qalanisi, Abu Ya`l6 Hamzah
ibn Asad, d. 1160.
The Damascus chronicle of the
Crusades.
Published/Created: New York:
AMS Press, [1980]
Editors: Gibb, H. A. R. (Hamilton
Alexander Rosskeen), Sir, 1895-
1971.
Description: 368 p.; 19 cm.
ISBN: 0404170196
Notes: Extracted and translated
from the Chronicle of Ibn al-
Qalanisi by H. A. R. Gibb.
Reprint of the 1932 ed. published
by Luzac, London, which was
issued as no. 5 of University of
London historical
Series. Includes indexes.
Subjects: Crusades. Damascus
(Syria)--History.
Series: University of London
historical
Series; no. 5.
LC Classification: D152 .I25213
1980
Dewey Class No.: 940.1/8
Language Code: eng ara

Ingebrand, Hermann, 1938-
Interpretationen zur
Kreuzzugslyrik Friedrichs von

Hausen, Albrechts von
Johansdorf, Heinrichs von Rugge,
Hartmanns von Aue und
Walthers von der Vogelweide.
Published/Created: [n.p.] 1966.
Description: 241 p. 21 cm.
Subjects: German poetry--Middle
High German--History and
criticism. Crusades in literature.
LC Classification: PT227 .I5

Jacoby, David.
Studies on the Crusader states
and on Venetian expansion /
David Jacoby.
Published/Created: Northampton
[England]: Variorum Reprints,
1989.
Description: 1 v. (various
pagings): ill., maps; 23 cm.
ISBN: 0860782492
Notes: Reprints of articles
published individually between
1979 and 1987. Includes
bibliographical references and
index.
Subjects: Crusades. Latin Orient-
-History. Venice (Italy)--History-
-697-1508.
Series: Collected studies; CS301.
Variant Series: Variorum reprint;
CS301
LC Classification: D179 .J3 1989

James, G. P. R. (George Payne
Rainsford), 1801?-1860.
The history of chivalry / by

G.P.R. James.
Published/Created: London: H.
Colburn and R. Bentley, 1830.
Description: xx, 348 p.: ill.; 18
cm.
Notes: Added t.p., engraved.
Subjects: Crusades. Chivalry.
Variant Series: The National
library; no. 4
LC Classification: D158 .J3 1830

Jammes, Francis, 1868-1938.
Saint Louis;
Published/Created: Paris, F.
Sorlot [1941]
Description: 2 p.l., [7]-158, [2] p.
incl. illus., plates. 19 cm.
Subjects: Louis IX, King of
France, 1214-1270. Crusades--
Seventh, 1248-1250.
LC Classification: DC91 .J3

Jeffery, George, d. 1935.
Cyprus under an English king in
the twelfth century; the
adventures of Richard I. and the
crowning of his queen in the
island.
Published/Created: London,
Zeno, 1973.
Description: 185 p. illus. 22 cm.
ISBN: 0900834773
Notes: Reprint of the 1926 ed.
Includes bibliographical
references.
Subjects: Richard I, King of
England, 1157-1199. Crusades--

Third, 1189-1192. British--
Cyprus--History--To 1500. Great
Britain--Kings and rulers--
Biography. Cyprus--History.
Variant Series: Bibliotheca
historica Cypria
LC Classification: D163.5.G7 J43
1973

Jerusalem: vision of peace [sound
    recording]
    Published/Created: London:
    Hyperion, p1998.
    Editors: Page, Christopher. cnd
    Guiot, de Dijon, 13th cent.
    Chanterai por mon corage. Huon,
    de Saint-Quentin, 13th cent.
    Jerusalem se plaint et li pans.
    Hildegard, Saint, 1098-1179.
    Symphonia armonie celestium
    revelationum O Jerusalem.
    Description: 1 sound disc: digital;
    4 3/4 in. Publisher Number:
    CDA67039 Hyperion
    Notes: "Songs and plainchants
    that may be connected in various
    ways with the crusades of the
    classic period, roughly 1180-
    1240"--Notes. For 1-6 voices,
    unacc. Compact disc. Program
    Notes in English, French, and
    German, and texts with English
    translations in container.
    Recorded 15-17 Jan. 1998,
    Boxgrove Priory, West Sussex.
    Sung in Latin or Old French.
    Cast: Gothic Voices; Christopher

Page, director.
    Subjects: Crusades--Songs and
    music. Chants (Plain, Gregorian,
    etc.) Motets.
    LC Classification: Hyperion
    CDA67039
    Language Code: latfro latfroeng
    latfro engfreger

Jessop, Joanne.
    Richard the Lionhearted / Joanne
    Jessop; illustrated by Martin
    Salisbury.
    Published/Created: New York:
    Bookwright Press, 1989.
    Editors: Salisbury, Martin.
    Description: 32 p.: ill. (some
    col.); 24 cm.
    ISBN: 0531182878 (lib. bdg.)
    Notes: Includes index.
    Bibliography: p. 30.
    Subjects: Richard I, King of
    England, 1157-1199 --Juvenile
    literature. Crusades--Third, 1189-
    1192--Juvenile literature. Great
    Britain--History--Richard I,
    1189-1199--Juvenile literature.
    Great Britain--Kings and rulers--
    Biography--Juvenile literature.
    Series: Great lives (New York,
    N.Y.)
    Variant Series: Great lives
    LC Classification: DA207 .J47
    1989

Jewett, Eleanore Myers.
    Big John's secret. With illus. by

Frederick T. Chapman.
Published/Created: New York,
Viking Press [1962]
Description: 236 p. illus. 21 cm.
Subjects: Crusades--Fifth, 1218-
1221--Juvenile fiction.
LC Classification: PZ7.J5533 Bi

Jews and Christians in twelfth-
century Europe / edited by
Michael A. Signer and John Van
Engen.
Published/Created: Notre Dame,
IN: University of Notre Dame
Press, c2001.
Editors: Signer, Michael Alan.
Van Engen, John H.
Description: xi, 380 p.: ill., maps;
24 cm.
ISBN: 026803253X (cl)
Notes: Includes bibliographical
references and index.
Subjects: Jews--Europe--History-
-To 1500--Congresses. Jews--
Germany--History--1096-1147--
Congresses. Crusades--First,
1096-1099--Jews--Congresses.
Christianity and other religions--
Judaism--Congresses. Judaism--
Relations--Christianity--
Congresses. Europe--Ethnic
relations--Congresses.
Series: Notre Dame conferences
in medieval studies; 10.
Variant Series: Notre Dame
conferences in medieval studies;
no. 10

LC Classification: DS124 .J52
2001
Dewey Class No.: 940/.04924 21

Jinks, Catherine.
Pagan's crusade / Catherine Jinks.
Published/Created: Sydney:
Hodder & Stoughton, 1993.
Description: 147 p.; 23 cm.
ISBN: 0195534859
Subjects: Crusades--Third, 1189-
1192--Juvenile fiction. Crusades-
-Third, 1189-1192--Fiction.
Knights and knighthood--Fiction.
Orphans--Fiction.
LC Classification: PZ7.J5754 Pag
1993
Dewey Class No.: [Fic] 20

John, Evan, 1901-1953.
Ride home tommorow; the
chronicle of a crusader newly set
forth by Evan John [pseud.]
Published/Created: London,
Heinemann [1950]
Description: vii, 468 p. 21 cm.
Notes: "Note on books": p. 466-
468.
Subjects: Crusades--Fiction.
LC Classification: PZ3.S6127 Ri

Joinville, Jean, sire de, 1224?-1317?
The history of St. Louis.
Translated from the French text
edited by Natalis de Wailly, by
Joan Evans.
Published/Created: London, New

York [etc.] Oxford University Press, 1938.
Editors: Wailly, Natalis de, 1805-1886, ed. Evans, Joan, 1893- , tr.
Description: xxviii, 281 p. illus. 23 cm.
Subjects: Louis IX, King of France, 1214-1270 Crusades--Seventh, 1248-1250.
LC Classification: DC91 .J7 1938
Language Code: engfre

Joinville, Jean, sire de, 1224?-1317?
The life of St. Louis / by John of Joinville; translated by René Hague from the text edited by Natalis de Wailly.
Published/Created: New York: Sheed and Ward, 1955.
Description: v, 306 p.: map; 22 cm.
Notes: Translation of: L'histoire et chronique du ... roy s. Loys. Includes bibliographic notes and index.
Subjects: Louis IX, King of France, 1214-1270. Crusades--Seventh, 1248-1250.
Variant Series: The Makers of Christendom
LC Classification: DC91 .J7 1955
Dewey Class No.: 923.144
Language Code: eng fre

Jones, Terry, 1942-
Crusades / Terry Jones and Alan Ereira.
Published/Created: New York, NY: Facts on File, c1995.
Editors: Ereira, Alan.
Description: 256 p.: ill., maps (some col.); 26 cm.
ISBN: 0816032750 (acid-free paper)
Notes: Includes bibliographical references (p. 248-250) and index.
Subjects: Crusades.
LC Classification: D157 .J66 1995
Dewey Class No.: 909.07 20

Jordan, William C., 1948-
Ideology and royal power in medieval France: kingship, crusades, and the Jews / William Chester Jordan.
Published/Created: Aldershot; Burlington, Vt.: Ashgate, c2001.
Description: 1 v. (various pagings): ill., map; 23 cm.
ISBN: 0860788563 (alk. paper)
Notes: Includes bibliographical references and index.
Subjects: Monarchy--France--History--To 1500. Crusades. Jews--France--History--To 1500. France--History--13th century. France--History--14th century.
Series: Collected studies; CS705.
Variant Series: Variorum collected studies Series; CS705
LC Classification: DC83 .J67

2001
Dewey Class No.: 944/.02 21

Jordan, William C., 1948-
Louis IX and the challenge of the Crusade: a study in rulership / William Chester Jordan.
Published/Created: Princeton, N.J.: Princeton University Press, c1979.
Description: xv, 291 p.: ill.; 25 cm.
ISBN: 0691052859
Notes: A revision of the author's thesis, Princeton, 1973, entitled: Saint Louis' influence on French Society and life in the thirteenth century. Includes index.
Bibliography: p. 253-282.
Subjects: Louis IX, King of France, 1214-1270. Crusades--Seventh, 1248-1250. Crusades--Eighth, 1270. France--History--Louis IX, 1226-1270.
LC Classification: DC91 .J75 1979
Dewey Class No.: 944/.023

Journeys toward God: pilgrimage and crusade / edited by Barbara N. Sargent-Baur.
Published/Created: Kalamazoo, Mich.: Medieval Institute Publications, Western Michigan University, 1992.
Editors: Sargent-Baur, Barbara Nelson.
Description: xii, 229 p.: ill., maps; 24 cm.
ISBN: 1879288036 1879288044 (pbk.)
Notes: Papers presented at a conference at the University of Pittsburgh, Oct. 27-28, 1988. Includes bibliographical references and index.
Subjects: Christian pilgrims and pilgrimages in literature Congresses. Crusades in literature--Congresses. Literature, Medieval--Themes, motives--Congresses. Christian pilgrims and pilgrimages--Europe--History Congresses. Crusades--History--Congresses.
Series: Studies in medieval culture; 30. Occasional studies Series (University of Pittsburgh. Medieval and Renaissance Studies Program); v. 5.
Variant Series: SMC; 30 Occasional studies Series / Medieval and Renaissance Studies Program of the University of Pittsburgh; v. 5
LC Classification: PN682.P5 J6 1992
Dewey Class No.: 809/.93355 20

Kay, Guy Gavriel.
A song for Arbonne / Guy Gavriel Kay.
Edition Information: 1st American ed.

Published/Created: New York:
Crown Publishers, c1992.
Description: 513 p.; 24 cm.
ISBN: 0517593122:
Subjects: Crusades--Fiction.
Middle Ages--Fiction.
Genre/Form: Love stories.
Historical fiction.
LC Classification: PR9199.3.K39
S6 1992
Dewey Class No.: 813/.54 20

Kedar, B. Z.
Crusade and mission: European
approaches toward the Muslims /
Benjamin Z. Kedar.
Published/Created: Princeton,
N.J.: Princeton University Press,
c1984.
Description: xiii, 246 p.; 25 cm.
ISBN: 069105424X (alk paper):
Notes: Includes index.
Bibliography: p. 229-239.
Subjects: Missions to Muslims.
Crusades. Europe--Relations--
Middle East. Middle East--
Relations--Europe.
LC Classification: BV2625 .K43
1984
Dewey Class No.:
266/.2/0917671 19

Kephart, Calvin, 1883-1969.
Origin of armorial insignia in
Europe; a contribution to
fundamental history, by Calvin
Kephart

Published/Created: Washington,
D.C., National Genealogical
Society, 1938.
Editors: Bowditch, Harold, 1883-
1964. Beginnings of armory.
Description: 11 p, 1 l., 10 p. 1
illus. 23 cm.
Notes: "Department of
Controversy and Correction. The
beginnings of armory, by Harold
Bowditch ...": 10 p. at end. "To
accompany publication entitled
Origin of armorial insignia in
Europe, by Calvin Kephart ...
1938. Reprinted, with slight
alterations, from New York
genealogical and biographical
record."--Leaf following p. 11.
Includes "References";
bibliographical footnotes.
Subjects: Armies--Insignia.
Crusades--First, 1096-1099.
Heraldry. Europe--History.
Variant Series: [National
Genealogical Society.
Genealogical publication no. 7]
LC Classification: UC530 .K4
Dewey Class No.: 355.13

Kephart, Calvin, 1883-1969.
Origin of heraldry in Europe, also
of miscellaneous surnames and
insignia: a contribution to
genealogy and history. Published
under the auspices of the National
Genealogical Society, on the
occasion of its jubilee (1903-

1953)
Edition Information: 2d ed.
Published/Created: Washington
[1953]
Description: 136 p. illus. 21 cm.
Notes: First ed. published in 1938
under Origin of armorial insignia
in Europe.
Subjects: Heraldry--History.
Crusades--First, 1096-1099.
LC Classification: CR151 .K4
1953
Dewey Class No.: 929.6

Kernaghan, Pamela.
The Crusades: cultures in conflict
/ Pamela Kernaghan.
Published/Created: New York,
NY, USA: Cambridge University
Press, 1993.
Description: 64 p.: ill. (some
col.), col. maps; 28 cm.
ISBN: 0521428467 0521446171
(pbk.)
Notes: Includes index.
Subjects: Crusades--Juvenile
literature. Crusades.
Series: Cambridge history
programme. Key stage 3.
Variant Series: Cambridge
history programme
LC Classification: D157 .K47
1993
Dewey Class No.: 909.07 20

Kerr, Anthony J. C.
The Crusades, by Anthony J. C.

Kerr; designed by Denis Wrigley,
illustrated by Neville Dear.
Published/Created: Exeter,
Wheaton, 1966.
Description: 95 p. illus. (some
col.) col. maps, diagrs. 22 1/2 cm.
Subjects: Crusades--Juvenile
literature.
LC Classification: D158 .K34
Dewey Class No.: 940.18

King Richard and the Crusaders
[Motion picture]
Published/Created: [n.p.] Warner
Bros. Pictures, 1954.
Editors: Scott, Walter, Sir, 1771-
1832. Talisman. Warner Brothers
Pictures, inc.
Description: p. 114 min., sd.,
color, 35 mm.
Notes: CinemScope.
Warnercolor. Based on the novel
The talisman, by Sir Walter Scott.
Subjects: Crusades--Third, 1189-
1192--Drama.

King, E. J. (Edwin James), Sir, 1877-
1952.
The Knights hospitallers in the
Holy Land, by Colonel E. J.
King.
Published/Created: London,
Methuen & co. ltd. [1931]
Description: xv, 336 p. plates,
ports., maps (1 fold.) plans. 23
cm.
Notes: Bibliography: p. xiii.

Subjects: Knights of Malta.
Crusades. Jerusalem--History--
Latin Kingdom, 1099-1244.
LC Classification: CR4723 .K47
Dewey Class No.: 929.711

Knowlton, Daniel Chauncey, 1876-
Christian Europe and the
Crusades.
Published/Created: Chicago, A. J.
Nystrom [1955]
Editors: Wallbank, Thomas
Walter, 1901- joint author.
Nystrom (A. J.) and Company,
Chicago.
Description: col. map 87 x 120
cm.
Subjects: Crusades--Maps.
Europe--Historical geography--
Maps. Middle East--Historical
geography--Maps.
LC Classification: G5701 .S3
1955.K5

Knox, Esther Melbourne.
Swift flies the falcon; a story of
the first crusade, by Esther
Milbourne Knox; illustrated by
Ruth King.
Published/Created: Philadelphia,
Chicago [etc.] The John
C.Winston company c1939.
Description: vii, 245 p., 1 l. illus.
23 cm.
Notes: Illustrated lining-papers.
"First edition." Bibliography: p.
245.

Subjects: Crusades--First, 1096-
1099--Fiction.
LC Classification: PZ7.K771 Sw

Kossak-Szczucka, Zofia, 1890-
Angels in the dust, a novel of the
First Crusade, by Zofia Kossak.
[Tr. by Rulka Langer and Lola
Gay-Tift]
Published/Created: New York,
Roy Publishers, 1947.
Editors: Langer, Rulka, tr.
Description: vi, 467 p. 21 cm.
Subjects: Crusades--First, 1096-
1099--Fiction.
LC Classification: PZ3.K847A N
Dewey Class No.: 891.853
Language Code: engpol

Krey, August Charles, 1887- ed. and
tr.
The first crusade;
Published/Created: Princeton,
Princeton university press; [etc.,
etc.] 1921.
Description: 3 p. l., v-viii, 299 p.
maps. 23 cm.
Subjects: Crusades--First, 1096-
1099.
LC Classification: D161.1.A3 K7

Lamb, Harold, 1892-1962.
The crusades ... by Harold Lamb.
Published/Created: Garden City,
N.Y., Doubleday, Doran &
company, inc., 1930-31.
Description: 2 v. fronts., plates,

ports., maps (1 fold.), plans, facsims. 24 cm.
Notes: "First edition." "Selected bibliography": [v. 1] p. [351]-358: [v. 2] p. [469]-475.
Subjects: Crusades. Latin Orient.
LC Classification: D157 .L3
Dewey Class No.: 940.18

Lamprey, Louise, 1869-1951.
The Treasure Valley, illustrated by Margaret Freeman.
Published/Created: New York, W. Morrow [c1928]
Description: xi, 337 p. incl. illus., plates. col. front., col. plates. 21 cm.
Notes: At head of L. Lamprey.
Bibliography: p. 337.
Subjects: Crusades--Third, 1189-1192--Fiction.
LC Classification: PZ8.1.L199 Tr

Lamprey, Louise, 1869-1951.
The Treasure Valley, illustrated by Margaret Freeman.
Published/Created: New York, W. Morrow [c1928]
Description: xi, 337 p. incl. illus., plates. col. front., col. plates. 21 cm.
Notes: At head of L. Lamprey.
Bibliography: p. 337.
Subjects: Crusades--Third, 1189-1192--Fiction.
LC Classification: PZ8.1.L199 Tr

Landau, Sol, 1920-
Christian-Jewish relations; a new era in Germany as the result of the First Crusade.
Edition Information: [1st ed.]
Published/Created: New York, Pageant Press [1960, c1959]
Description: 78 p. 21 cm.
Notes: Includes bibliography.
Subjects: Jews--Germany--History. Crusades--First, 1096-1099.
LC Classification: DS135.G31 L3

Landau, Sol, 1920-
Christian-Jewish relations; a new era in Germany as the result of the First Crusade.
Edition Information: [1st ed.]
Published/Created: New York, Pageant Press [1960, c1959]
Description: 78 p. 21 cm.
Notes: Includes bibliography.
Subjects: Jews--Germany--History. Crusades--First, 1096-1099.
LC Classification: DS135.G31 L3

Lasky, Kathryn.
Robin Hood: the boy who became a legend / by Kathryn Lasky.
Published/Created: New York: Blue Sky Press, 1998. Projected Pub. Date: 9804

Description: p. cm.
ISBN: 0590259334
Subjects: Robin Hood
(Legendary character)--Juvenile
fiction. Robin Hood (Legendary
character)--Fiction. Falconry--
Fiction. Hawks--Fiction. Great
Britain--History--Richard I,
1189-1199--Juvenile fiction.
Great Britain--History--Richard I,
1189-1199--Fiction.
LC Classification: PZ7.L3274 Ro
1998
Dewey Class No.: [Fic] 21

Lasky, Kathryn.
Robin Hood: the boy who
became a legend / by Kathryn
Lasky.
Published/Created: New York:
Blue Sky Press, 1998. Projected
Pub. Date: 9804
Description: p. cm.
ISBN: 0590259334
Subjects: Robin Hood
(Legendary character)--Juvenile
fiction. Robin Hood (Legendary
character)--Fiction. Falconry--
Fiction. Hawks--Fiction. Great
Britain--History--Richard I,
1189-1199--Juvenile fiction.
Great Britain--History--Richard I,
1189-1199--Fiction.
LC Classification: PZ7.L3274 Ro
1998
Dewey Class No.: [Fic] 21

Lawhead, Steve.
The black rood / Stephen R.
Lawhead.
Edition Information: 1st ed.
Published/Created: New York:
EOS, c2000.
Description: 437 p.: maps; 25
cm.
ISBN: 0061050342 (alk. paper)
Subjects: Christian antiquities--
Fiction. Scots--Middle East--
Fiction. Crusades--Fiction.
Jerusalem--History--Latin
Kingdom, 1099-1244--Fiction.
Scotland--History--1057-1603--
Fiction. Middle East--Fiction.
Genre/Form: Historical fiction.
Series: Lawhead, Steve. Celtic
crusades; v. 2.
Variant Series: The Celtic
crusades; bk. 2
LC Classification: PS3562.A865
B58 2000
Dewey Class No.: 813/.54 21

Lawhead, Steve.
The black rood / Stephen R.
Lawhead.
Edition Information: 1st ed.
Published/Created: New York:
EOS, c2000.
Description: 437 p.: maps; 25
cm.
ISBN: 0061050342 (alk. paper)
Subjects: Christian antiquities--
Fiction. Scots--Middle East--
Fiction. Crusades--Fiction.

Jerusalem--History--Latin
Kingdom, 1099-1244--Fiction.
Scotland--History--1057-1603--
Fiction. Middle East--Fiction.
Genre/Form: Historical fiction.
Series: Lawhead, Steve. Celtic
crusades; v. 2.
Variant Series: The Celtic
crusades; bk. 2
LC Classification: PS3562.A865
B58 2000
Dewey Class No.: 813/.54 21

Lawhead, Steve.
The iron lance / Stephen R.
Lawhead.
Edition Information: 1st U.S. ed.
Published/Created: New York:
HarperPrism/Zondervan, c1998.
Description: 498 p.: maps; 25
cm.
ISBN: 0061050326
Subjects: Crusades--First, 1096-
1099--Fiction. Christian
antiquities--Fiction. Scots--
Middle East--Fiction. Scotland--
History--1057-1603--Fiction.
Middle East--Fiction.
Genre/Form: Historical fiction.
Fantasy fiction.
Series: Lawhead, Steve. Celtic
crusades; v. 1.
Variant Series: The Celtic
crusades; v. 1
LC Classification: PS3562.A865
I76 1998

Dewey Class No.: 813/.54 21

Lawhead, Steve.
The iron lance / Stephen R.
Lawhead.
Edition Information: 1st U.S. ed.
Published/Created: New York:
HarperPrism/Zondervan, c1998.
Description: 498 p.: maps; 25
cm.
ISBN: 0061050326
Subjects: Crusades--First, 1096-
1099--Fiction. Christian
antiquities--Fiction. Scots--
Middle East--Fiction. Scotland--
History--1057-1603--Fiction.
Middle East--Fiction.
Genre/Form: Historical fiction.
Fantasy fiction.
Series: Lawhead, Steve. Celtic
crusades; v. 1.
Variant Series: The Celtic
crusades; v. 1
LC Classification: PS3562.A865
I76 1998
Dewey Class No.: 813/.54 21

Lawrence, T. E. (Thomas Edward),
1888-1935.
Crusader castles / by T.E.
Lawrence.
Edition Information: A new ed. /
with introduction and notes by
Denys Pringle.
Published/Created: Oxford
[England]: Clarendon Press;
New York: Oxford University

Press, 1988.
Editors: Pringle, Denys.
Description: xl, 154 p.: ill., maps;
25 cm.
ISBN: 019822964X:
Notes: Includes bibliographical
references and index.
Subjects: Fortification--Middle
East--History. Fortification--
Great Britain--History. Castles--
Great Britain--History.
Fortification--France--History.
Castles--Middle East--History.
Castles--France--History.
Crusades.
LC Classification: UG432.M628
L38 1988
Dewey Class No.: 355.7/09 19

Lawrence, T. E. (Thomas Edward),
1888-1935.
Crusader castles / by T.E.
Lawrence.
Edition Information: A new ed. /
with introduction and notes by
Denys Pringle.
Published/Created: Oxford
[England]: Clarendon Press;
New York: Oxford University
Press, 1988.
Editors: Pringle, Denys.
Description: xl, 154 p.: ill., maps;
25 cm.
ISBN: 019822964X:
Notes: Includes bibliographical
references and index.
Subjects: Fortification--Middle

East--History. Fortification--
Great Britain--History. Castles--
Great Britain--History.
Fortification--France--History.
Castles--Middle East--History.
Castles--France--History.
Crusades.
LC Classification: UG432.M628
L38 1988
Dewey Class No.: 355.7/09 19

Leopold, Antony, 1972-
How to recover the Holy Land:
the crusade proposals of the late
thirteenth and early fourteenth
centuries / Antony Leopold.
Published/Created: Aldershot,
England; Burlington, VT:
Ashgate, c2000.
Description: x, 231 p.; 24 cm.
ISBN: 075460120X (alk. paper)
Notes: Abstract of thesis (Ph.D.)-
-University of Durham, 1998.
Includes bibliographical
references (p. [208]-221) and
index.
Subjects: Crusades--Later, 13th,
14th, and 15th centuries. Church
history--Middle Ages, 600-1500.
Papacy--History--To 1309.
Middle East--History. Christans--
Latin Orient. Byzantine Empire--
History--1081-1453. Jerusalem--
History--Latin Kingdom, 1099-
1244.
LC Classification: D171 .L46
2000

Dewey Class No.: 909.07 21

Leopold, Antony, 1972-
How to recover the Holy Land:
the crusade proposals of the late
thirteenth and early fourteenth
centuries / Antony Leopold.
Published/Created: Aldershot,
England; Burlington, VT:
Ashgate, c2000.
Description: x, 231 p.; 24 cm.
ISBN: 075460120X (alk. paper)
Notes: Abstract of thesis (Ph.D.)-
-University of Durham, 1998.
Includes bibliographical
references (p. [208]-221) and
index.
Subjects: Crusades--Later, 13th,
14th, and 15th centuries. Church
history--Middle Ages, 600-1500.
Papacy--History--To 1309.
Middle East--History. Christans--
Latin Orient. Byzantine Empire--
History--1081-1453. Jerusalem--
History--Latin Kingdom, 1099-
1244.
LC Classification: D171 .L46
2000
Dewey Class No.: 909.07 21

Lesourd, Paul, 1897-
On the path of the crusaders, by
Paul Lesourd and Jean Marie
Ramiz. Edited by Miriam
Ismojik. Translated from the
French by Jerry O'Dell.
Published/Created: [Ramat-Gan]
Massada Press [c1969]
Editors: Ramiz, Jean-Marie, joint
author.
Description: 276 p. illus. (part
col.) 28 cm.
Subjects: Crusades.
LC Classification: D157 .L43
Dewey Class No.: 940.1/8
Language Code: engfre

Lesourd, Paul, 1897-
On the path of the crusaders, by
Paul Lesourd and Jean Marie
Ramiz. Edited by Miriam
Ismojik. Translated from the
French by Jerry O'Dell.
Published/Created: [Ramat-Gan]
Massada Press [c1969]
Editors: Ramiz, Jean-Marie, joint
author.
Description: 276 p. illus. (part
col.) 28 cm.
Subjects: Crusades.
LC Classification: D157 .L43
Dewey Class No.: 940.1/8
Language Code: engfre

Lilie, Ralph-Johannes.
Byzantium and the crusader
states, 1096-1204 / by Ralph-
Johannes Lilie; translated by J.C.
Morris and Jean E. Ridings.
English Edition Information:
Rev. 1988.
Published/Created: Oxford:
Clarendon Press; New York:
Oxford University Press, 1993.

Description: ix, 342 p.: maps; 24 cm.
ISBN: 0198204078
Notes: Includes bibliographical references (p. [321]-336) and index.
Subjects: Crusades. Byzantine Empire--Foreign relations--Latin Orient. Latin Orient--Foreign relations--Byzantine Empire. Byzantine Empire--Foreign relations--1081-1453.
LC Classification: DF547.L37 L5413 1993
Dewey Class No.: 949.5/03 20
Language Code: eng ger

Lilie, Ralph-Johannes.
Byzantium and the crusader states, 1096-1204 / by Ralph-Johannes Lilie; translated by J.C. Morris and Jean E. Ridings.
English Edition Information: Rev. 1988.
Published/Created: Oxford: Clarendon Press; New York: Oxford University Press, 1993.
Description: ix, 342 p.: maps; 24 cm.
ISBN: 0198204078
Notes: Includes bibliographical references (p. [321]-336) and index.
Subjects: Crusades. Byzantine Empire--Foreign relations--Latin Orient. Latin Orient--Foreign relations--Byzantine Empire.

Byzantine Empire--Foreign relations--1081-1453.
LC Classification: DF547.L37 L5413 1993
Dewey Class No.: 949.5/03 20
Language Code: eng ger

Lincoln, Henry.
The holy place: discovering the eighth wonder of the ancient world / Henry Lincoln.
Edition Information: 1st U.S. ed.
Published/Created: New York: Arcade Pub., c1991.
Description: 176 p.: ill. (some col.); 26 cm.
ISBN: 1559701234:
Notes: Includes bibliographical references (p. 175).
Subjects: Jesus Christ--Relics of the Nativity. Templars. Relics--France--Rennes-le-Chateau. Crusades. Rennes-le-Chateau (France)--History--Miscellanea.
LC Classification: DC801.R42 L56 1991
Dewey Class No.: 944/.87 20

Lincoln, Henry.
The holy place: discovering the eighth wonder of the ancient world / Henry Lincoln.
Edition Information: 1st U.S. ed.
Published/Created: New York: Arcade Pub., c1991.
Description: 176 p.: ill. (some col.); 26 cm.

ISBN: 1559701234:
Notes: Includes bibliographical
references (p. 175).
Subjects: Jesus Christ--Relics of
the Nativity. Templars. Relics--
France--Rennes-le-Chateau.
Crusades. Rennes-le-Chateau
(France)--History--Miscellanea.
LC Classification: DC801.R42
L56 1991
Dewey Class No.: 944/.87 20

Lloyd, S. D. (Simon D.)
English society and the crusade,
1216-1307 / Simon Lloyd.
Published/Created: Oxford:
Clarendon Press; New York:
Oxford University Press, 1988.
Description: xiii, 329 p.: ill.; 22
cm.
ISBN: 0198229496:
Notes: Series statement from jkt.
Revision of thesis (Ph. D.)--
Oxford University, 1983.
Includes index. Bibliography: p.
[285]-305.
Subjects: Crusades--Later, 13th,
14th, and 15th centuries. Social
history--Medieval, 500-1500.
Great Britain--History--13th
century. Great Britain--History--
Edward I, 1272-1307. England--
Social conditions--1066-1485.
Series: Oxford historical
monographs
LC Classification: DA225 .L56
1988

Dewey Class No.: 940.1/84 19

Lloyd, S. D. (Simon D.)
English society and the crusade,
1216-1307 / Simon Lloyd.
Published/Created: Oxford:
Clarendon Press; New York:
Oxford University Press, 1988.
Description: xiii, 329 p.: ill.; 22
cm.
ISBN: 0198229496:
Notes: Series statement from jkt.
Revision of thesis (Ph. D.)--
Oxford University, 1983.
Includes index. Bibliography: p.
[285]-305.
Subjects: Crusades--Later, 13th,
14th, and 15th centuries. Social
history--Medieval, 500-1500.
Great Britain--History--13th
century. Great Britain--History--
Edward I, 1272-1307. England--
Social conditions--1066-1485.
Series: Oxford historical
monographs
LC Classification: DA225 .L56
1988
Dewey Class No.: 940.1/84 19

Lock, Peter, 1949-
The Franks in the Aegean, 1204-
1500 / Peter Lock.
Published/Created: London; New
York: Longman, 1995.
Description: xiii, 400 p.: ill.,
maps; 24 cm.
ISBN: 0582051401 (case)

0582051398 (pbk.)
Notes: Includes bibliographical references (p. 338-355) and index.
Subjects: Franks--Aegean Sea Region--History. Crusades--Later, 13th, 14th, and 15th centuries. Civilization, Aegean--Foreign influences. Byzantine Empire--History--1081-1453.
LC Classification: DF609 .L63 1995
Dewey Class No.: 949.5/02 20

Lock, Peter, 1949-
The Franks in the Aegean, 1204-1500 / Peter Lock.
Published/Created: London; New York: Longman, 1995.
Description: xiii, 400 p.: ill., maps; 24 cm.
ISBN: 0582051401 (case) 0582051398 (pbk.)
Notes: Includes bibliographical references (p. 338-355) and index.
Subjects: Franks--Aegean Sea Region--History. Crusades--Later, 13th, 14th, and 15th centuries. Civilization, Aegean--Foreign influences. Byzantine Empire--History--1081-1453.
LC Classification: DF609 .L63 1995
Dewey Class No.: 949.5/02 20

Ludlow, James Meeker, 1841-
The age of the crusades,
Published/Created: New York, The Christian literature co., 1896.
Description: p. cm.
Subjects: Crusades.
LC Classification: BR141 .T4 vol. VI

Ludlow, James Meeker, 1841-
The age of the crusades,
Published/Created: New York, The Christian literature co., 1896.
Description: p. cm.
Subjects: Crusades.
LC Classification: BR141 .T4 vol. VI

Lurier, Harold E.
The Crusades; [Sound recording] a lecture by Harold Lurier.
Published/Created: [n.p.] Listening Library PC 3377. 1969.
Description: p. 4 s. 12 in. 33 1/3 rpm. microgroove.
Notes: Let's go to class Series. Read by the author. Text of the lecture (10 p.) laid in container; notes on container.
Subjects: Crusades.

Lurier, Harold E.
The Crusades; [Sound recording] a lecture by Harold Lurier.
Published/Created: [n.p.] Listening Library PC 3377. 1969.
Description: p. 4 s. 12 in. 33 1/3

rpm. microgroove.
Notes: Let's go to class
Series. Read by the author. Text
of the lecture (10 p.) laid in
container; notes on container.
Subjects: Crusades.

Luttrell, Anthony, 1932-
Latin Greece, the Hospitallers,
and the Crusades, 1291-1440 /
Anthony Luttrell.
Published/Created: London:
Variorum Reprints, 1982.
Description: 322 p. in various
pagings: ports.; 23 cm.
ISBN: 0860781062
Notes: English, Italian, and
Spanish. Reprint of previously
published articles. Includes
bibliographical references and
index.
Subjects: Hospitalers. Crusades--
Later, 13th, 14th, and 15th
centuries. Greece--History--323-
1453. Latin Orient--History.
Series: Variorum reprint; CS158
LC Classification: BX2825 .L88
1982
Dewey Class No.: 133.8 19
Language Code: engitaspa

Luttrell, Anthony, 1932-
Latin Greece, the Hospitallers,
and the Crusades, 1291-1440 /
Anthony Luttrell.
Published/Created: London:
Variorum Reprints, 1982.

Description: 322 p. in various
pagings: ports.; 23 cm.
ISBN: 0860781062
Notes: English, Italian, and
Spanish. Reprint of previously
published articles. Includes
bibliographical references and
index.
Subjects: Hospitalers. Crusades--
Later, 13th, 14th, and 15th
centuries. Greece--History--323-
1453. Latin Orient--History.
Series: Variorum reprint; CS158
LC Classification: BX2825 .L88
1982
Dewey Class No.: 133.8 19
Language Code: engitaspa

Maalouf, Amin.
The crusades through Arab eyes /
Amin Maalouf; translated by Jon
Rothschild.
English Edition Information: 1st
American ed.
Published/Created: New York:
Schocken Books, 1985.
Description: xvi, 293 p.: maps;
21 cm.
ISBN: 0805240047
Notes: Translation of: Les
croisades vues par les Arabes.
Includes index. Bibliography: p.
[267]-276.
Subjects: Crusades. Islamic
Empire--History--750-1258.
LC Classification: DS38.6
.M3213 1985

Dewey Class No.: 909/.09767101
19
Language Code: engfre

Maalouf, Amin.
The crusades through Arab eyes /
Amin Maalouf; translated by Jon
Rothschild.
English Edition Information: 1st
American ed.
Published/Created: New York:
Schocken Books, 1985.
Description: xvi, 293 p.: maps;
21 cm.
ISBN: 0805240047
Notes: Translation of: Les
croisades vues par les Arabes.
Includes index. Bibliography: p.
[267]-276.
Subjects: Crusades. Islamic
Empire--History--750-1258.
LC Classification: DS38.6
.M3213 1985
Dewey Class No.: 909/.09767101
19
Language Code: engfre

Macquarrie, Alan.
Scotland and the crusades, 1095-
1560 / Alan Macquarrie.
Published/Created: Edinburgh: J.
Donald Publishers; Atlantic
Highlands, NJ, USA: Exclusive
distribution in the U.S.A. and
Canada by Humanities Press,
c1985.
Description: xiii, 154 p.; 24 cm.

ISBN: 0859761150
Notes: Includes index.
Bibliography: p. 135-146.
Subjects: Crusades. Scotland--
History--1057-1603.
LC Classification: D160 .M33
1985
Dewey Class No.: 940.1/7 19

Macquarrie, Alan.
Scotland and the crusades, 1095-
1560 / Alan Macquarrie.
Published/Created: Edinburgh: J.
Donald Publishers; Atlantic
Highlands, NJ, USA: Exclusive
distribution in the U.S.A. and
Canada by Humanities Press,
c1985.
Description: xiii, 154 p.; 24 cm.
ISBN: 0859761150
Notes: Includes index.
Bibliography: p. 135-146.
Subjects: Crusades. Scotland--
History--1057-1603.
LC Classification: D160 .M33
1985
Dewey Class No.: 940.1/7 19

Madden, Thomas F.
A concise history of the Crusades
/ Thomas F. Madden.
Published/Created: Lanham, Md.:
Rowman & Littlefield, c1999.
Description: xi, 249 p.: ill.; 24
cm.
ISBN: 0847694291
Notes: Includes bibliographical

references (p. 221-232) and index.
Subjects: Crusades.
Series: Critical issues in history
LC Classification: D157 .M33 1999
Dewey Class No.: 909.07 21

Madden, Thomas F.
A concise history of the Crusades / Thomas F. Madden.
Published/Created: Lanham, Md.: Rowman & Littlefield, c1999.
Description: xi, 249 p.: ill.; 24 cm.
ISBN: 0847694291
Notes: Includes bibliographical references (p. 221-232) and index.
Subjects: Crusades.
Series: Critical issues in history
LC Classification: D157 .M33 1999
Dewey Class No.: 909.07 21

Maier, Christoph T.
Preaching the Crusades: mendicant friars and the Cross in the thirteenth century / Christoph T. Maier.
Published/Created: Cambridge; New York: Cambridge University Press, 1994.
Description: x, 202 p.; 23 cm.
ISBN: 0521452465
Notes: Based on the author's thesis (Ph. D.)--University of

London, 1990. Includes bibliographical references (p. 175-190) and index.
Subjects: Friars--Europe--History. Crusades--Later, 13th, 14th, and 15th centuries.
Preaching--History--Middle Ages, 600-1500.
Series: Cambridge studies in medieval life and thought; 4th ser., 28
LC Classification: BX2820 .M33 1994
Dewey Class No.: 270.5 20

Maier, Christoph T.
Preaching the Crusades: mendicant friars and the Cross in the thirteenth century / Christoph T. Maier.
Published/Created: Cambridge; New York: Cambridge University Press, 1994.
Description: x, 202 p.; 23 cm.
ISBN: 0521452465
Notes: Based on the author's thesis (Ph. D.)--University of London, 1990. Includes bibliographical references (p. 175-190) and index.
Subjects: Friars--Europe--History. Crusades--Later, 13th, 14th, and 15th centuries.
Preaching--History--Middle Ages, 600-1500.
Series: Cambridge studies in medieval life and thought; 4th

ser., 28
LC Classification: BX2820 .M33
1994
Dewey Class No.: 270.5 20

Marshall, Christopher.
Warfare in the Latin East, 1192-
1291 / Christopher Marshall.
Published/Created: Cambridge;
New York: Cambridge University
Press, 1992.
Description: xi, 290 p.: ill., maps;
22 cm.
ISBN: 0521394287
Notes: Includes bibliographical
references (p. 272-280) and
index.
Subjects: Crusades. Jerusalem--
History--Latin Kingdom, 1099-
1244. Jerusalem--History,
Military.
Series: Cambridge studies in
medieval life and thought: 4th
ser.
LC Classification: D183 .M37
1991
Dewey Class No.: 956.94/03 20

Marshall, Christopher.
Warfare in the Latin East, 1192-
1291 / Christopher Marshall.
Published/Created: Cambridge;
New York: Cambridge University
Press, 1992.
Description: xi, 290 p.: ill., maps;
22 cm.
ISBN: 0521394287

Notes: Includes bibliographical
references (p. 272-280) and
index.
Subjects: Crusades. Jerusalem--
History--Latin Kingdom, 1099-
1244. Jerusalem--History,
Military.
Series: Cambridge studies in
medieval life and thought: 4th
ser.
LC Classification: D183 .M37
1991
Dewey Class No.: 956.94/03 20

Martell, Hazel.
The Normans / Hazel Mary
Martell.
Edition Information: 1st ed.
Published/Created: New York:
New Discovery Books, 1992.
Description: 64 p.: col. ill.; 25
cm.
ISBN: 0027624285
Subjects: Normandy, Dukes of--
Juvenile literature. Normans--
France--Social life and customs--
Juvenile literature. Crusades--
Juvenile literature. Normans.
Normandy (France)--History--To
1515--Juvenile literature.
Series: Worlds of the past
LC Classification: DC611.N862
M37 1992
Dewey Class No.: 942.02 20

Martell, Hazel.
The Normans / Hazel Mary

Martell.
Edition Information: 1st ed.
Published/Created: New York:
New Discovery Books, 1992.
Description: 64 p.: col. ill.; 25
cm.
ISBN: 0027624285
Subjects: Normandy, Dukes of--
Juvenile literature. Normans--
France--Social life and customs--
Juvenile literature. Crusades--
Juvenile literature. Normans.
Normandy (France)--History--To
1515--Juvenile literature.
Series: Worlds of the past
LC Classification: DC611.N862
M37 1992
Dewey Class No.: 942.02 20

Mastnak, Tomaz.
Crusading peace: Christendom,
the Muslim world, and Western
political order / Tomaz Mastnak.
Published/Created: Berkeley:
University of California Press,
2002. Projected Pub. Date: 0201
Description: p. cm.
ISBN: 0520226356 (alk. paper)
Notes: Includes bibliographical
references (p.) and index.
Subjects: Catholic Church--
Doctrines--History--Middle
Ages, 600-1500. Crusades.
Peace--Religious aspects--
Christianity--History of
doctrines--Middle Ages, 600-
1500. Just war--Doctrine--
History--To 1500. Monarchy--
Europe--History--To 1500.
Peace--Religious aspects--Islam.
Europe--Church history--600-
1500.
LC Classification: D157 .M376
2002
Dewey Class No.: 909.07 21

Mastnak, Tomaz.
Crusading peace: Christendom,
the Muslim world, and Western
political order / Tomaz Mastnak.
Published/Created: Berkeley:
University of California Press,
2002. Projected Pub. Date: 0201
Description: p. cm.
ISBN: 0520226356 (alk. paper)
Notes: Includes bibliographical
references (p.) and index.
Subjects: Catholic Church--
Doctrines--History--Middle
Ages, 600-1500. Crusades.
Peace--Religious aspects--
Christianity--History of
doctrines--Middle Ages, 600-
1500. Just war--Doctrine--
History--To 1500. Monarchy--
Europe--History--To 1500.
Peace--Religious aspects--Islam.
Europe--Church history--600-
1500.
LC Classification: D157 .M376
2002
Dewey Class No.: 909.07 21

Matthew, of Edessa, 12th cent.
Armenia and the Crusades: tenth
to twelfth centuries: the
Chronicle of Matthew of Edessa /
translated from the original
Armenian with a commentary
and introduction by Ara Edmond
Dostourian; foreword by Krikor
H. Maksoudian.
Published/Created: [Belmont,
MA?]: National Association for
Armenian Studies and Research;
Lanham: University Press of
America, c1993.
Editors: Dostourian, Ara
Edmond. Grigor, Erets`, 12th
cent.
Description: xiii, 375 p.: maps;
24 cm.
ISBN: 0819189537 (cloth: alk.
paper)
Notes: By Matthew of Edessa,
continued by Grigor Erets`.
Includes bibliographical
references (p. [365]) and index.
Subjects: Crusades. Armenia--
History--Turkic Mongol
domination, 1045-1592.
Armenia--History--Bagratuni
dynasty,885-1045. Islamic
Empire--History--750-1258.
Series: Armenian heritage
Series
LC Classification: DS186
.M3713 1993
Dewey Class No.: 956.6/2013 20

Language Code: eng arm

Matthew, of Edessa, 12th cent.
Armenia and the Crusades: tenth
to twelfth centuries: the
Chronicle of Matthew of Edessa /
translated from the original
Armenian with a commentary
and introduction by Ara Edmond
Dostourian; foreword by Krikor
H. Maksoudian.
Published/Created: [Belmont,
MA?]: National Association for
Armenian Studies and Research;
Lanham: University Press of
America, c1993.
Editors: Dostourian, Ara
Edmond. Grigor, Erets`, 12th
cent.
Description: xiii, 375 p.: maps;
24 cm.
ISBN: 0819189537 (cloth: alk.
paper)
Notes: By Matthew of Edessa,
continued by Grigor Erets`.
Includes bibliographical
references (p. [365]) and index.
Subjects: Crusades. Armenia--
History--Turkic Mongol
domination, 1045-1592.
Armenia--History--Bagratuni
dynasty,885-1045. Islamic
Empire--History--750-1258.
Series: Armenian heritage
Series
LC Classification: DS186
.M3713 1993

Dewey Class No.: 956.6/2013 20
Language Code: eng arm

Mayer, H. E. (Hans Eberhard), 1932-
The Crusades / by Hans Eberhard
Mayer; translated by John
Gillingham.
English Edition Information: 2nd
ed.
Published/Created: Oxford; New
York: Oxford University Press,
1988.
Description: ix, 354 p.: maps; 23
cm.
ISBN: 0198730985: 0198730977
(pbk.):
Notes: Rev. translation of the
origianl German ed. published in
1965 under Geschichte der
Kreuzzьge. Includes index.
Bibliography: p. [289]-322.
Subjects: Crusades.
LC Classification: D157 .M3813
1988
Dewey Class No.: 940.1/8 19
Language Code: engger

Mayer, H. E. (Hans Eberhard), 1932-
The Crusades / by Hans Eberhard
Mayer; translated by John
Gillingham.
English Edition Information: 2nd
ed.
Published/Created: Oxford; New
York: Oxford University Press,
1988.
Description: ix, 354 p.: maps; 23
cm.
ISBN: 0198730985: 0198730977
(pbk.):
Notes: Rev. translation of the
origianl German ed. published in
1965 under Geschichte der
Kreuzzьge. Includes index.
Bibliography: p. [289]-322.
Subjects: Crusades.
LC Classification: D157 .M3813
1988
Dewey Class No.: 940.1/8 19
Language Code: engger

Meakin, Nevill Myers, 1876-
The assassins; a romance of the
crusades.
Published/Created: New York, H.
Holt and co., 1902.
Description: vi, 426 p. 20 cm.
Subjects: Assassins--Fiction.
Crusades--Third, 1189-1192--
Fiction.
LC Classification: PZ3.M462 A

Meakin, Nevill Myers, 1876-
The assassins; a romance of the
crusades.
Published/Created: New York, H.
Holt and co., 1902.
Description: vi, 426 p. 20 cm.
Subjects: Assassins--Fiction.
Crusades--Third, 1189-1192--
Fiction.
LC Classification: PZ3.M462 A
Michaud, J. Fr. (Joseph Fr.), 1767-
1839.

Michaud's history of the crusades. Tr. from the French, by W. Robson.
Published/Created: London, G. Routledge and co., 1852.
Editors: Robson, William, 1785-1863, tr.
Description: 3 v. front., 3 fold. maps. 18 cm.
Subjects: Crusades.
LC Classification: D157 .M62
Language Code: freeng

Michaud, J. Fr. (Joseph Fr.), 1767-1839.
Michaud's history of the crusades. Tr. from the French, by W. Robson.
Published/Created: London, G. Routledge and co., 1852.
Editors: Robson, William, 1785-1863, tr.
Description: 3 v. front., 3 fold. maps. 18 cm.
Subjects: Crusades.
LC Classification: D157 .M62
Language Code: freeng

Michaud, J. Fr. (Joseph Fr.), 1767-1839.
The history of the crusades. Translated from the French, by W. Robson ...
Published/Created: New York, Redfield, 1853.
Editors: Robson, William, 1785-1863.

Description: 3 v. fronts. (fold. maps) 19 cm.
Subjects: Crusades.
LC Classification: D157 .M62 1953
Language Code: eng fre

Michaud, J. Fr. (Joseph Fr.), 1767-1839.
The history of the crusades. Translated from the French, by W. Robson ...
Published/Created: New York, Redfield, 1853.
Editors: Robson, William, 1785-1863.
Description: 3 v. fronts. (fold. maps) 19 cm.
Subjects: Crusades.
LC Classification: D157 .M62 1953
Language Code: eng fre

Millar, Bonnie.
The siege of Jerusalem in its physical, literary, and historical contexts / Bonnie Millar.
Published/Created: Dublin; Portland, OR: Four Courts Press, c2000.
Description: 251 p.; 25 cm.
ISBN: 1851825061
Notes: Appendix (p. 233-240) contains two passages from the poem transcribed by the author from the extant manuscripts. Includes bibliographical

references and index.
Subjects: Siege of Jerusalem
(Middle English poem) Literature
and history--History--To 1500.
Romances, English--History and
criticism. Mother and child in
literature. Antisemitism in
literature. Cannibalism in
literature. Crusades in literature.
Sieges in literature. Jerusalem--
History--Siege, 701 B.C.--
Historiography. Jerusalem--In
literature.
Series: Medieval studies
LC Classification: PR2065.S53
M55 2000
Dewey Class No.: 821/.1 21

Millar, Bonnie.
The siege of Jerusalem in its
physical, literary, and historical
contexts / Bonnie Millar.
Published/Created: Dublin;
Portland, OR: Four Courts Press,
c2000.
Description: 251 p.; 25 cm.
ISBN: 1851825061
Notes: Appendix (p. 233-240)
contains two passages from the
poem transcribed by the author
from the extant manuscripts.
Includes bibliographical
references and index.
Subjects: Siege of Jerusalem
(Middle English poem) Literature
and history--History--To 1500.
Romances, English--History and
criticism. Mother and child in
literature. Antisemitism in
literature. Cannibalism in
literature. Crusades in literature.
Sieges in literature. Jerusalem--
History--Siege, 701 B.C.--
Historiography. Jerusalem--In
literature.
Series: Medieval studies
LC Classification: PR2065.S53
M55 2000
Dewey Class No.: 821/.1 21

Mombert, J. I. (Jacob Isidor), 1829-
1913.
A short history of the crusades by
J. I. Mombert, D.D.
Published/Created: New York, D.
Appleton and co., 1894.
Description: 3 p. l., 301 p. 2 fold.
maps. 18 cm.
Notes: "Brief list of authorities":
p. 294.
Subjects: Crusades.
LC Classification: D158 .M73

Mombert, J. I. (Jacob Isidor), 1829-
1913.
A short history of the crusades by
J. I. Mombert, D.D.
Published/Created: New York, D.
Appleton and co., 1894.
Description: 3 p. l., 301 p. 2 fold.
maps. 18 cm.
Notes: "Brief list of authorities":
p. 294.
Subjects: Crusades.

LC Classification: D158 .M73

Morgan, Margaret Ruth.
The Chronicle of Ernoul and the
Continuations of William of
Tyre, by M. R. Morgan.
Published/Created: [London]
Oxford University Press, 1973.
Description: 204 p. 22 cm.
ISBN: 0198218516
Notes: Based on the author's
thesis [Oxford University].
Bibliography: p. [196]-202.
Subjects: Ernoul, fl. 1187.
Chronique d'Ernoul et de Bernard
de Trésorier. William, of Tyre,
Archbishop of Tyre, ca. 1130-ca.
1190. Historia rerum in partibus
transmarinis gestarum. Godfrey,
of Bouillon, ca. 1060-1100.
Crusades--First, 1096-1099--
Sources. Jerusalem--History--
Latin Kingdom, 1099-1244--
Sources.
Variant Series: Oxford historical
monographs
LC Classification: D152.E73
M67
Dewey Class No.: 940.1/8

Morgan, Margaret Ruth.
The Chronicle of Ernoul and the
Continuations of William of
Tyre, by M. R. Morgan.
Published/Created: [London]
Oxford University Press, 1973.
Description: 204 p. 22 cm.

ISBN: 0198218516
Notes: Based on the author's
thesis [Oxford University].
Bibliography: p. [196]-202.
Subjects: Ernoul, fl. 1187.
Chronique d'Ernoul et de Bernard
de Trésorier. William, of Tyre,
Archbishop of Tyre, ca. 1130-ca.
1190. Historia rerum in partibus
transmarinis gestarum. Godfrey,
of Bouillon, ca. 1060-1100.
Crusades--First, 1096-1099--
Sources. Jerusalem--History--
Latin Kingdom, 1099-1244--
Sources.
Variant Series: Oxford historical
monographs
LC Classification: D152.E73
M67
Dewey Class No.: 940.1/8

On crusade: more tales of the Knights
Templar / edited by Katherine
Kurtz.
Published/Created: New York:
Warner Books, 1998.
Editors: Kurtz, Katherine.
Description: x, 246 p.; 21 cm.
ISBN: 0446673390
Notes: Includes bibliographical
references (p. [241]).
Subjects: Templars--Fiction.
Historical fiction, American.
Crusades--Fiction.
LC Classification: PS648.T45 O5
1998
Dewey Class No.:

813/.0108382557913 21

Outremer: studies in the history of the crusading kingdom of Jerusalem presented to Joshua Prawer / edited by B.Z. Kedar, H.E. Mayer, R.C. Smail.
Published/Created: Jerusalem: Yad Izhak Ben-Zvi Institute, 1982.
Editors: Prawer, Joshua. Kedar, B. Z. Mayer, H. E. (Hans Eberhard), 1932- Smail, R. C. Yad Yitshak Ben-Tsevi.
Description: 346 p.: ill.; 24 cm.
ISBN: 9652170100
Notes: Includes bibliographical references.
Subjects: Prawer, Joshua. Crusades. Jerusalem--History--Latin Kingdom, 1099-1244.
LC Classification: D159 .O9 1982
Dewey Class No.: 909.07 19

Queller, Donald E.
Medieval diplomacy and the Fourth Crusade / Donald E. Queller.
Published/Created: London: Variorum Reprints, 1980.
Description: [323] p.: port.; 24 cm.
ISBN: 0860780597:
Notes: English and French. Includes bibliographical references and index.

Subjects: Diplomacy--History--To 1500. Crusades--Fourth, 1202-1204. Europe--Foreign relations.
Series: Variorum reprint; CS114.
Variant Series: Collected studies Series; CS 114
LC Classification: JX1641 .Q42
Dewey Class No.: 327.2/094 19
Language Code: engfre

Queller, Donald E.
The Fourth Crusade: the conquest of Constantinople / Donald E. Queller and Thomas F. Madden; with an essay on primary sources by Alfred J. Andrea.
Edition Information: 2nd [rev.] ed.
Published/Created: Philadelphia: University of Pennsylvania Press, c1997.
Editors: Madden, Thomas F.
Description: xi, 357 p.: maps; 24 cm.
ISBN: 0812233875 (acid-free paper)
Notes: Includes bibliographical references (p. [299]-343) and index.
Subjects: Crusades--Fourth, 1202-1204. Istanbul (Turkey)--History--Siege, 1203-1204.
Series: The Middle Ages Series
LC Classification: D164 .Q38 1997

Dewey Class No.: 949.61/8013
21

Queller, Donald E., comp.
The Latin conquest of
Constantinople. Edited by Donald
E. Queller.
Published/Created: New York,
Wiley [1971]
Description: xv, 113 p. map. 22
cm.
ISBN: 0471702471
Subjects: Crusades--Fourth,
1202-1204.
Variant Series: Major issues in
history
LC Classification: D164 .Q4
Dewey Class No.: 940.1/8

Quinn, Vernon, 1881-1962.
The march of iron men; the tale
of the crusades, by Vernon
Quinn...with frontispiece in color
by H.C. Murphy and four
illustrations by Richard H.
Rodgers.
Published/Created: New York,
Frederick A. Stokes company,
1930.
Description: xii p., 2 l., 303 p.
incl. illus., plates, map. col. front.
20 cm.
Notes: Maps on lining-papers.
Subjects: Crusades--Fiction.
LC Classification: PZ7.Q42 Mar

Regan, Geoffrey.
Lionhearts: Saladin, Richard I,
and the era of the Third Crusade /
Geoffrey Regan.
Published/Created: New York:
Walker, 1999.
Description: xxv, 254 p.: ill.,
maps; 24 cm.
ISBN: 0802713548
Notes: Originally published:
Great Britain, 1998. Includes
bibliographical references (p.
239-244) and index.
Subjects: Saladin, Sultan of
Egypt and Syria, 1137-1193.
Richard I, King of England,
1157-1199. Crusades--Third,
1189-1192. Great Britain--
History--Richard I, 1189-1199.
LC Classification: D163 .R44
1999
Dewey Class No.: 956/.014 21

Rennell, James Rennell Rodd, Baron,
1858-1941.
The princes of Achaia and the
Chronicles of Morea, a study of
Greece in the middle ages, by Sir
Rennell Rodd ...
Published/Created: London, E.
Arnold, 1907.
Description: 2 v. fold. map,
geneal. tables. 23 cm.
Notes: "Introduction: Historical
authorities": v. 1, p. 1-25.
Subjects: Crusades--Fourth,
1202-1204. Achaia (Principality)-

-1205-1430.
LC Classification: DF623 .R4
Dewey Class No.: 949.5

Reston, James, 1941-
Warriors of God: Richard the
Lionheart and Saladin in the
Third Crusade / James Reston, Jr.
Edition Information: 1st ed.
Published/Created: New York:
Doubleday, 2001.
Description: xx, 364 p., [16] p. of
plates: ill., maps; 24 cm.
ISBN: 0385495617
Notes: Includes bibliographical
references (p. 347-354) and
index.
Subjects: Richard I, King of
England, 1157-1199 Saladin,
Sultan of Egypt and Syria, 1137-
1193 Crusades--Third, 1189-
1192. Jerusalem--History--Latin
Kingdom, 1099-1244.
LC Classification: D163.4 .R47
2001
Dewey Class No.: 942.03/2/092
B 21

Richard, Jean, 1921 Feb. 7-
The Crusades, c. 1071-c. 1291 /
Jean Richard; translated by Jean
Birrell.
Published/Created: Cambridge,
U.K.; New York, NY:
Cambridge University Press,
c1999.
Description: xiv, 516 p.: maps,
geneal. tables; 23 cm.
ISBN: 0521623693 hb
0521625661 pb
Notes: Includes bibliographical
references (p. 492-502) and
index.
Subjects: Crusades.
Series: Cambridge medieval
textbooks
LC Classification: D157 .R52413
1999
Dewey Class No.: 909.07 21
Language Code: eng fre

Richard, the Lion Hearted / Cines.
Published/Created: Italy: Cines,
[1912?].
Editors: Cines (Firm) AFI/Poston
(Tom) Collection (Library of
Congress)
Description: 1 reel of 1 (370 ft.):
si., b&w; 16 mm. ref print. 1 reel
of 1 (935 ft.): si., b&w; 35 mm.
ref print. 1 reel of 1 (906 ft.): si.,
b&w; 35 mm. dupe neg.
Notes: Copyright: no reg. Minor
change version: [English
language interior titles]. -- United
States: Cines, 1912. The film was
probably originally entitled Il
Talismano and released in 1911
in Italy. LC 16 mm. print is the
better copy, having less
deterioration than the 35 mm.
print, which also has the film
switch one-third through so that
the intertitles are backwards.

Based on the novel, The Talisman, by Sir Walter Scott. NCN016911; Richard the lion-hearted. Source used: Moving picture world, v. 12, p. 1022, 1075, v. 13, 906; Prolo, Storia del cinema muto Italiano, v. 1, p. 142. Source of Acquisition: Received: 7/12/79 from LC film lab; 16 mm. ref print; preservation; AFI/Poston (Tom) Collection. Received: 5/16/79 from LC film lab; 35 mm. ref print; preservation; AFI/Poston (Tom) Collection. Received: 2/3/75 from LC film lab; dupe neg; preservation; AFI/Poston (Tom) Collection. Genre/Form: Adventure--Short. Adaptation--Short.
LC Classification: FAB 7235 (ref print) FEB 6103 (ref print) FPB 4161 (dupe neg)

Riley-Smith, Jonathan Simon
    Christopher, 1938-
    The atlas of the Crusades /
    Jonathan Riley-Smith.
    Published/Created: New York:
    Facts on File, 1991, c1990.
    Editors: Swanston Graphics
    Limited.
    Description: 1 atlas (192 p.): col.
    ill., col. maps; 29 cm.
    ISBN: 0816021864 Scale
    Information: Scale not given.
    Notes: "Maps, illustrations and

typesetting by Swanston Graphics, Derby"--Verso t.p. Includes bibliographical references (p. 173), index and glossary. Subjects: Crusades--Maps. Geography, Medieval--Maps. LC Classification: G1034 .R5 1990
Dewey Class No.: 911 20

Riley-Smith, Jonathan Simon
    Christopher, 1938-
    The Crusades: a short history /
    Jonathan Riley-Smith.
    Published/Created: New Haven
    [Conn.]: Yale University Press,
    1987.
    Description: xxx, 302 p.: maps;
    24 cm.
    ISBN: 0300039050
    Notes: Includes index.
    Bibliography: p. [259]-273.
    Subjects: Crusades.
    LC Classification: D157 .R53
    1987
    Dewey Class No.: 909.07 19

Riley-Smith, Jonathan Simon
    Christopher, 1938-
    The First Crusade and the idea of
    crusading / Jonathan Riley-Smith.
    Published/Created: Philadelphia:
    University of Pennsylvania Press,
    1986.
    Description: 227 p.: maps; 23
    cm.

ISBN: 0812280261 (alk. paper)
Notes: Includes index.
Bibliography: p. [204]-213.
Subjects: Crusades--First, 1096-1099. Crusades. Church history--Middle Ages, 600-1500.
Series: The Middle Ages
LC Classification: D161.2 .R48 1986
Dewey Class No.: 940.1/8 19

Riley-Smith, Jonathan Simon Christopher, 1938-
The first crusaders, 1095-1131 / Jonathan Riley-Smith.
Published/Created: Cambridge, U.K.; New York, NY, USA: Cambridge University Press, 1997.
Description: x, 300 p.: ill., maps; 24 cm.
ISBN: 0521590051 (hardcover)
Notes: Includes bibliographical references (p. 251-274) and index.
Subjects: Crusades--First, 1096-1099.
LC Classification: D161.2 .R485 1997
Dewey Class No.: 940.1/8 20

Riley-Smith, Jonathan Simon Christopher, 1938-
What were the Crusades? / Jonathan Riley-Smith.
Published/Created: Totowa, N.J.: Rowman and Littlefield, 1977.

Description: 92 p.; 23 cm.
ISBN: 0874719445
Notes: Includes index.
Bibliography: p. [81]-84.
Subjects: Crusades.
LC Classification: D157 .R54 1977
Dewey Class No.: 909.07

Rivele, Stephen J., 1949-
A booke of days: a novel of the Crusades / Stephen J. Rivele.
Edition Information: 1st pbk. ed.
Published/Created: New York: Carroll & Graf Publishers, 1998.
Projected Pub. Date: 9803
Description: p. cm.
ISBN: 0786704624
Subjects: Crusades--First, 1096-1099--Fiction. Genre/Form: Historical fiction.
LC Classification: PS3568.I8286 B6 1998
Dewey Class No.: 813/.54 21

Robert de Clari, fl 1200-1216.
The conquest of Constantinople
Published/Created: New York, Columbia university press, 1936.
Editors: McNeal, Edgar Holmes, 1874- tr.
Description: 5 p. l., [3]-150 p. illus. (map) 24 cm.
Subjects: Crusades--Fourth, 1202-1204. Istanbul (Turkey)--History--Siege, 1203-1204.

LC Classification: D164.A3 R62

Ross, Stewart.
    A crusading knight / Stewart
    Ross; illustrated by Mark Bergin.
    Published/Created: Vero Beach,
    Fla.: Rourke Enterprises, 1987,
    c1986.
    Editors: Bergin, Mark, ill.
    Description: [32] p.: ill. (some
    col.); 24 cm.
    ISBN: 0865921423
    Notes: Includes index.
    Subjects: Crusades--Juvenile
    literature. Knights and
    knighthood--Europe--Juvenile
    literature. Crusades. Knights and
    knighthood.
    Series: How they lived
    LC Classification: D160 .R67
    1987
    Dewey Class No.: 909.07 19

Rowling, Marjorie.
    Everyday life of medieval
    travellers. Drawings by John
    Mansbridge.
    Published/Created: London, B. T.
    Batsford; New York, G. P.
    Putnam's Sons [1971]
    Description: 208 p. illus., maps.
    22 cm.
    ISBN: 0713416866
    Notes: Bibliography: p. 198-202.
    Subjects: Travel, Medieval--
    Juvenile literature. Travel,
    Medieval.

Variant Series: [Everyday life
Series]
LC Classification: G369 .R68
1971
Dewey Class No.: 914/.03/17

Runciman, Steven, Sir, 1903-
    A history of the Crusades.
    Edition Information: [1st ed.]
    Published/Created: Cambridge
    [Eng.] University Press, 1951-54.
    Description: 3 v. illus., ports.,
    maps, fold. geneal. table. 22 cm
    Subjects: Crusades.
    LC Classification: D157 .R8
    Dewey Class No.: 940.18

Runciman, Steven, Sir, 1903-
    The First Crusade / Steven
    Runciman.
    Edition Information: Canto ed.
    Published/Created: Cambridge
    [England]; New York:
    Cambridge University Press,
    1992.
    Description: vi, 201 p.; 22 cm.
    ISBN: 0521427053 (pbk.)
    Notes: "First published as volume
    1 of The history of the crusades,
    1951; this abridged edition first
    published 1980"--T.p. verso.
    Includes index.
    Subjects: Crusades--First, 1096-
    1099.
    LC Classification: D161.2 .R862
    1992

Dewey Class No.: 940.1/8 20

Saunders, J. J. (John Joseph), 1910-
1972.
Aspects of the Crusades [by] J. J.
Saunders.
Edition Information: [2d ed.]
Published/Created:
[Christchurch] Whitcombe &
Tombs [1969]
Description: 91 p. 22 cm.
Notes: "The literature of the
Crusades.": p. [9]-20 Includes
bibliographical references.
Subjects: Crusades.
LC Classification: D159 .S28
1969
Dewey Class No.: 909.07

Schmandt, Raymond Henry, 1925-
The crusades; origin of an
ecumenical problem [by]
Raymond H. Schmandt.
Published/Created: Houston,
University of Saint Thomas
[1967]
Description: 38 p. port. 15 cm.
Notes: At head of The Smith
lecture under the auspices of the
History Dept., University of Saint
Thomas. Bibliographical
footnotes.
Subjects: Crusades. Church
history--Middle Ages, 600-1500.
Series: The Smith lecture, 1967
Variant Series: The Smith history
lecture, 1967

LC Classification: D159 .S35
Dewey Class No.: 940.1/8

Schoonover, Lawrence L.
The golden exile.
Published/Created: New York,
Macmillan, 1951.
Description: 392 p. 22 cm.
Subjects: Arnaldus, de Villanova,
d. 1311 --Fiction. Crusades--
Later, 13th, 14th, and 15th
centuries--Fiction.
LC Classification: PZ3.S3728 Go

Scott, Walter, Sir, 1771-1832.
The talisman; a tale of the
crusaders, by Sir Walter Scott,
bart.; ed. with an introduction by
Julia M. Dewey.
Published/Created: New York,
Cincinnati [etc.] American Book
Company [c1899]
Description: 304 p. 19 cm.
Subjects: Crusades--Third, 1189-
1192--Fiction.
Series: Eclectic school readings
LC Classification: PZ3.S43 Tal21

Setton, Kenneth Meyer, 1914-
A history of the Crusades. Editor-
in-chief: Kenneth M. Setton.
Published/Created: [Philadelphia]
University of Pennsylvania Press
[1955-62]
Description: 2 v. illus., col. maps.
26 cm.
Subjects: Crusades.

LC Classification: D157 .S48
Dewey Class No.: 940.18

Setton, Kenneth Meyer, 1914-
The Papacy and the Levant,
1204-1571 / Kenneth M. Setton.
Published/Created: Philadelphia:
American Philosophical Society,
1976-1984.
Description: 4 v.; 28 cm.
ISBN: 0871691140 (v. 1)
Notes: Includes bibliographical
references and indexes.
Subjects: Papacy--History.
Crusades. Middle East--History.
Series: Memoirs of the American
Philosophical Society; v. 114,
etc.
Variant Series: Memoirs of the
American Philosophical Society;
v. 114, 127, 161-162 0065-9738
LC Classification: Q11 .P612 vol.
114, etc. BX955.2
Dewey Class No.: 081 s 270.5

Severin, Timothy.
Crusader: by horse to Jerusalem /
Tim Severin; photographs by
Peter Essick.
Published/Created: London:
Hutchinson, 1989.
Description: 338 p., [24] p. of
plates: ill. (some col.); 24 cm.
ISBN: 0091735157
Notes: Includes index. Includes
bibliographical references (p.
327).

Subjects: Severin, Timothy--
Journeys. Crusades--First, 1096-
1099. Middle East--
Description and travel. Europe,
Eastern--
Description and travel.
LC Classification: DS49.7 .S45
1989
Dewey Class No.: 915.604/5 20

Shaw, Margaret R. B. (Margaret
Renée Bryers), ed. and tr.
Chronicles of the Crusades.
Published/Created: Baltimore,
Penguin Books [1963]
Editors: Villehardouin, Geoffroi
de, d. ca. 1212. Conquest of
Constantinople. Joinville, Jean,
sire de, 1224?-1317? Life of
Saint Louis.
Description: 362 p. maps. 18 cm.
Subjects: Crusades.
Series: The Penguin classics,
L124
LC Classification: D151 .S5
Dewey Class No.: 940.18
Language Code: eng und

Shwartz, Susan, 1949-
Cross and crescent / Susan
Shwartz.
Edition Information: 1st ed.
Published/Created: New York:
TOR, 1997.
Description: 382 p.; 22 cm.
ISBN: 0312857144 (acid-free
paper)

Notes: "A Tom Doherty Associates book."
Subjects: Alexius I Comnenus, Emperor of the East, 1048-1118 Fiction. Crusades--First, 1096-1099--Fiction. Byzantine Empire--History--Alexius I Comnenus, 1081-1118 Fiction. Genre/Form: Historical fiction. Fantastic fiction.
LC Classification: PS3569.H873 C76 1997
Dewey Class No.: 813/.54 21

Siberry, Elizabeth.
Criticism of crusading: 1095-1274 / Elizabeth Siberry.
Published/Created: Oxford [Oxfordshire]: Clarendon Press; New York: Oxford University Press, 1985.
Description: xii, 257 p.; 23 cm.
ISBN: 0198219539:
Notes: Includes index.
Bibliography: p. [221]-245.
Subjects: Crusades--Historiography. Middle Ages--Historiography.
LC Classification: D160 .S49 1985
Dewey Class No.: 909.07 19

Siberry, Elizabeth.
The new crusaders: images of the crusades in the nineteenth and early twentieth centuries / Elizabeth Siberry.

Published/Created: Aldershot; Burlington USA: Ashgate, c2000.
Description: xii, 228 p.: ill.; 24 cm.
ISBN: 1859283330 (hb)
Notes: Includes bibliographical references (p. [212]-220) and index.
Subjects: Crusades--Historiography.
Series: Nineteenth century (Aldershot, England)
Variant Series: The nineteenth century
LC Classification: D156.58 .S53 2000
Dewey Class No.: 909.07 21

Siedschlag, Beatrice Nina, 1908-
English participation in the crusades, 1150-1220, by Beatrice N. Siedschlag.
Published/Created: [Menasha, Wis.] Priv. print. [The Collegiate press, George Banta pub. co.] 1939.
Description: viii, 173 p., 1 l. 23 cm.
Notes: Vita. Thesis (Ph. D) - Bryn Mawr college, 1937.
Bibliography: p. [149]-161.
Subjects: Crusades. Great Britain--History--Angevin period, 1154-1216.
LC Classification: D163 .5G7S55 1937

Sienkiewicz, Henryk, 1846-1916.
The knights of the cross, by
Henryk Sienkiewicz ...
Authorized and unabridged
translation from the Polish, by
Jeremiah Curtin ...
Published/Created: Boston, Little,
Brown, and Company, 1900.
Editors: Curtin, Jeremiah, 1835-
1906, tr.
Description: 2 v. front. (port.) 21
cm.
Subjects: Teutonic Knights--
History--Fiction. Crusades--
Fiction. Poland--History--
Jagellons, 1386-1572--Fiction.
LC Classification: PZ3.S57 K8
Language Code: engpol

Sivan, Emmanuel.
Modern Arab historiography of
the Crusades / E. Sivan.
Published/Created: [Tel-Aviv]:
Tel Aviv University, Shiloah
Center for Middle Eastern and
African Studies, 1973.
Description: 64 p.; 22 cm.
Notes: Includes bibliographical
references.
Subjects: Crusades--
Historiography.
Series: Occasional papers
(Mekhon Shiloah le-heker ha-
Mizrah ha-Tikhon ve-Afrikah)
(Unnumbered)
Variant Series: Occasional papers
- Shiloah Center for Middle

Eastern and African Studies
LC Classification: D156.58 .S58
Dewey Class No.: 909.07

Slack, Corliss Konwiser, 1955-
Crusade charters, 1138-1270 /
Corliss Konwiser Slack; with
English translations by Hugh
Bernard Feiss.
Published/Created: Tempe:
Arizona Center for Medieval and
Renaissance Studies, 2001.
Description: xxx, 229 p.: ill.; 24
cm.
ISBN: 0866982396 (alk. paper)
Notes: Includes bibliographical
references (p. [207]-225) and
index. Introd. in English; the
charters are in Latin, with English
translations.
Subjects: Crusades--Sources.
Charters.
Series: Medieval & Renaissance
Texts & Studies (
Series); v. 197.
Variant Series: Medieval and
Renaissance texts and studies; v.
197
LC Classification: D151 .S6 2001
Dewey Class No.: 909.07 21
Language Code: englat lat

Smail, R. C.
Crusading warfare, 1097-1193 /
R.C. Smail.
Edition Information: 2nd ed.
Published/Created: Cambridge

[England]; New York, NY, USA: Cambridge University Press, 1995.
Description: xxxiv, 276 p.: ill., maps; 22 cm.
ISBN: 0521480299 (hardback) 0521458382 (pbk.)
Notes: Includes bibliographical references (p. [251]-265) and index.
Subjects: Crusades. Military art and science--History--Medieval, 500-1500.
Series: Cambridge studies in medieval life and thought
LC Classification: D160 .S55 1995
Dewey Class No.: 940.1/8 20

Smail, R. C.
The crusaders; in Syria and the Holy Land [by] R. C. Smail.
Published/Created: New York, Praeger [1974, c1973]
Description: 232 p. illus. 21 cm.
Notes: Bibliography: p. 188-191.
Subjects: Crusades. Latin Orient.
Variant Series: Ancient peoples and places, v. 82
LC Classification: D183 .S5 1974
Dewey Class No.: 915.691

Smith, Arthur D. Howden (Arthur Douglas Howden), 1887-1945.
Spears of destiny; a story of the first capture of Constantinople, by Arthur D. Howden Smith ...
Published/Created: New York, George H. Doran Company [c1919]
Description: viii p., 1 l., 9-342 p. 20 cm.
Subjects: Crusades--Fourth, 1202-1204--Fiction. Istanbul (Turkey)--History--Siege, 1203-1204--Fiction.
LC Classification: PZ3.S6431 Sp

Stebbin, Henry, 1799-1883.
The history of chivalry and the crusades.
Published/Created: Edinburgh, Printed for Constable and co.; [etc., etc.] 1830.
Description: 2 v. 16 cm.
Subjects: Crusades. Chivalry.
LC Classification: D158 .S81

Steffens, Bradley, 1956-
The Children's Crusade / by Bradley Steffens.
Published/Created: San Diego, Calif.: Lucent Books, c1991.
Description: 64 p.: ill., map; 24 cm.
ISBN: 1560060190:
Notes: Includes bibliographical references (p. 60) and index.
Subjects: Children's Crusade, 1212--Juvenile literature.
Children's Crusade, 1212.
Crusades.
Series: World disasters
LC Classification: D169 .S74

1991
Dewey Class No.: 940.1/8 20

Stein, Evaleen.
Our little crusader cousin of long
ago; being the story of Hugo,
page to King Richard of England,
in the third crusade,
Published/Created: Boston, The
Page company, 1921.
Description: xiv p., 2 l., 144 p.
col. front., plates. 20 cm.
Subjects: Crusades--Third, 1189-
1192--Fiction.
LC Classification: PZ9.S819 Ocr

Stone, Edward Noble, 1870- tr.
Three Old French chronicles of
the crusades: the History of the
holy war, the History of them that
took Constantinople, the
Chronicle of Reims. Translated
into English by Edward Noble
Stone.
Published/Created: Seattle,
Wash., The University of
Washington, 1939.
Editors: Ambroise, fl. ca. 1196.
Histoire de la guerre sainte.
Robert de Clari, fl. 1200-1216.
La conquкte de Constantinople.
Description: 1 p. l., v-vii, 377 p.
26 cm.
Subjects: Crusades. Middle Ages-
-History. France--History--
Capetians, 987-1328. Istanbul
(Turkey)--History--Siege, 1203-

1204.
Variant Series: University of
Washington publications in the
social sciences. v. 10
LC Classification: D151 .S8
Dewey Class No.: 940.18
Language Code: engfre

Stubbs, William, bp. of Oxford,
1825-1901, ed.
Chronicles and memorials of the
reign of Richard I ...
Published/Created: London,
Longman, Roberts, and Green,
1864-65.
Editors: Ricardus, canonicus
Sanctae Trinitatis londoniensis.
Osbernus, 12th cent., supposed
author. Neophytus, Saint, fl.
1190-1216. Canterbury, Eng.
Christ church priory.
Description: 2 v. 25 cm.
Subjects: Crusades--Third, 1189-
1192. Great Britain--History--
Richard I, 1189-1199.
LC Classification: DA25 .B5 no.
38

Sturtevant, Peleg
Orondalie: a tale of the crusades.
Published/Created: Hudson [N.Y.]
P. Sturtevant, 1825.
Description: 56 p. 24 cm.
Subjects: Crusades--Poetry.
LC Classification: PS2962 .S7307

Suskind, Richard.
  Cross and crescent: the story of
  the crusades. Illustrated by Victor
  Lazzaro.
  Edition Information: [1st ed.]
  Published/Created: New York,
  Norton [1967]
  Description: 82 p. illus., map. 24
  cm.
  Subjects: Crusades--Juvenile
  literature.
  LC Classification: D158 .S93
  Dewey Class No.: 909.07

Suskind, Richard.
  The Crusades.
  Published/Created: New York:
  Ballantine Books [1962]
  Description: 192 p. illus. 18 cm.
  Subjects: Crusades.
  Variant Series: Ballatine books,
  F573
  LC Classification: D158 .S94

Sybel, Heinrich von, 1817-1895.
  The history and literature of the
  crusades. From the German of
  von Sybel. Edited by Lady Duff
  Gordon.
  Published/Created: London,
  Chapman and Hall, 1861.
  Editors: Duff Gordon, Lucie,
  Lady, 1821-1869, editor.
  Description: viii, 356 p. 20 cm.
  Subjects: Crusades. Crusades--
  Bibliography.
  LC Classification: D158 .S98

Language Code: engger

Tarr, Judith.
  Pride of kings / Judith Tarr.
  Published/Created: New York:
  RoC, c2001.
  Description: 451 p.; 23 cm.
  ISBN: 0451458478 (alk. paper)
  Subjects: Richard I, King of
  England, 1157-1199 --Fiction.
  Crusades--First, 1096-1099--
  Fiction. Great Britain--History--
  Richard I, 1189-1199--Fiction.
  Genre/Form: Alternative histories
  (Fiction) Fantasy fiction.
  LC Classification: PS3570.A655
  P75 2001
  Dewey Class No.: 813/.54 21

Tasso, Torquato, 1544-1595.
  Godfrey of Bulloigne: a critical
  edition of Edward Fairfax's
  translation of Tasso's
  Gerusalemme liberata, together
  with Fairfax's original poems /
  edited by Kathleen M. Lea and T.
  M. Gang.
  Published/Created: Oxford:
  Clarendon Press; New York:
  Oxford University Press, 1981.
  Editors: Fairfax, Edward, d.
  1635. Lea, Kathleen Marguerite.
  Gang, T. M.
  Description: x, 707 p., [3] leaves
  of plates: ill.; 23 cm.
  ISBN: 0198124805:
  Notes: Includes bibliographical

references and index.
Subjects: Godfrey, of Bouillon,
ca. 1060-1100 --Poetry. Epic
poetry, Italian--Translations into
English. Crusades, First, 1096-
1099--Poetry. Jerusalem--
History--Latin Kingdom, 1099-
1244--Poetry.
LC Classification: PQ4642.E21
F3 1981
Dewey Class No.: 851/.4
Language Code: engita

Tasso, Torquato, 1544-1595.
Jerusalem delivered: an English
prose version / Torquato Tasso;
translated and edited by Ralph
Nash.
Published/Created: Detroit:
Wayne State University Press,
1987.
Editors: Nash, Ralph, 1925-
Description: xxv, 511 p.: 1 ill.;
24 cm.
ISBN: 0814318290 0814318304
(pbk.)
Notes: Translation of:
Gerusalemme liberata. Includes
index. Bibliography: p. [497]-
499.
Subjects: Godfrey, of Bouillon,
ca. 1060-1100 --Poetry. Epic
poetry, Italian--Translations into
English. Crusades, First, 1096-
1099--Poetry. Jerusalem--
History--Latin Kingdom, 1099-
1244--Poetry.

.

LC Classification: PQ4642.E21
N37 1987
Dewey Class No.: 851/.4 19
Language Code: engita

Tate, Georges.
The crusaders: warriors of God /
Georges Tate; [translated from
the French by Lory Frankel].
Published/Created: New York,
N.Y.: Abrams, c1996.
Description: 191 p.: ill. (some
col.); 18 cm.
ISBN: 0810928299 (pbk.):
Notes: Includes bibliographical
references and index.
Subjects: Crusades.
Series: Discoveries (New York,
N.Y.)
Variant Series: Discoveries
LC Classification: D157 .T3713
1996
Dewey Class No.: 909.07 21
Language Code: eng fre

Thatcher, Oliver J. (Oliver Joseph),
1857-1937.
Mohammed, mohammedanism,
and the crusades: syllabus of a
course of six lecture-studies / by
Oliver J. Thatcher.
Published/Created: Chicago:
University of Chicago Press,
1894-
Editors: YA Pamphlet Collection
(Library of Congress)
Description: v. <2; 20 cm.

Subjects: Crusades.
Variant Series: The University of Chicago, University Extension Division, Lecture-Study Department; no. 64
LC Classification: YA 24472

The 1000s / Brenda Stalcup, book editor.
Published/Created: San Diego, Calif.: Greenhaven Press, c2001.
Editors: Stalcup, Brenda.
Description: 314 p.: ill., maps; 24 cm.
ISBN: 0737705272 (pbk.: alk. paper) 0737705280 (lib.: alk. paper)
Notes: Includes bibliographical references (p. 299-303) and index.
Subjects: Eleventh century. Civilization, Medieval. Middle Ages--History. Crusades--First, 1096-1099. Indians--History. Asia--History.
Series: Headlines in history
LC Classification: CB354.3 .A16 2001
Dewey Class No.: 940.1/46 21

The conquest of Jerusalem and the Third Crusade: sources in translation / Peter W. Edbury.
Published/Created: Brookfield, Vt.: Scolar Press, c1996.
Editors: Edbury, P. W. (Peter W.) William, of Tyre, Archbishop of Tyre, ca. 1130-ca. 1190. Historia rerum in partibus transmarinis gestarum. English.
Description: 196 p.; 25 cm.
ISBN: 1859282911
Subjects: Crusades--Third, 1189-1192--Sources. Jerusalem--History--Latin Kingdom, 1099-1244--Sources.
LC Classification: D163.A3 C66 1996
Dewey Class No.: 909.07 20
Language Code: eng fro

The Crusades / Brenda Stalcup, book editor.
Published/Created: San Diego, Calif.: Greenhaven Press, c2000.
Editors: Stalcup, Brenda.
Description: 258 p.; 23 cm.
ISBN: 1565109937 (lib. bdg.: alk. paper) 1565109929 (pbk.: alk. paper)
Notes: Includes bibliographical references (p. 249-251) and index.
Subjects: Crusades.
Series: Turning points in world history (Greenhaven Press)
Variant Series: Turning points in world history
LC Classification: D159 .C787 2000
Dewey Class No.: 909.07 21

The Crusades [Filmstrip]
Published/Created: [n.p.] Popular

Science Pub. Co., 1954.
Editors: Popular Science
Publishing Company, inc., New
York.
Description: p. 45 fr., folor, 35
mm.
Notes: America's Old World
background. Ansco color. With
teacher's guide.
Subjects: Crusades.

The Crusades and early trade routes
[Filmstrip]
Published/Created: [n.p.] Jam
Handy Organization, 1953.
Editors: (Jam) Handy
Organization, inc.
Description: p. 17 fr., color, 35
mm.
Notes: Age of discovery and
exploration, no. 1. Ansco color.
Captioned maps.
Subjects: Crusades--Maps. Trade
routes.
Series: Age of discovery and
exploration [Filmstrip] no. 1.

The crusades and their sources:
essays presented to Bernard
Hamilton / edited by John France
and William G. Zajac.
Published/Created: Aldershot,
Hampshire, Great Britain;
Brookfield, Vt.: Ashgate, 1998.
Editors: Hamilton, Bernard,
1932- France, John. Zajac,
William G.

Description: xix, 297 p.: ill.; 24
cm.
ISBN: 0860786242 (acid-free
paper)
Notes: "Bibliography of books
and articles by Bernard Hamilton,
1961-1996"--P. xv-xix. Includes
bibliographical references and
index. Includes two contributions
in French and one in German.
Subjects: Crusades--Sources.
LC Classification: D151 .C78
1998
Dewey Class No.: 909.07 21
Language Code: engfreger

The Crusades from the perspective of
Byzantium and the Muslim world
/ edited by Angeliki E. Laiou and
Roy Parviz Mottahedeh.
Published/Created: Washington,
D.C.: Dumbarton Oaks Research
Library and Collection, c2001.
Editors: Laiou, Angeliki E.
Mottahedeh, Roy P., 1940-
Description: vi, 297 p.: ill.; 26
cm.
ISBN: 0884022773 (alk. paper)
Notes: Includes bibliographical
references and index.
Subjects: Crusades. Civilization,
Eastern.
LC Classification: D160 .B99
2001
Dewey Class No.: 909.07 21

The Crusades, and other historical essays; presented to Dana C. Munro by his former students. Edited by Louis J. Paetow. Published/Created: Freeport, N.Y., Books for Libraries Press [1968, c1928] Editors: Munro, Dana Carleton, 1866-1933. Paetow, Louis John, 1880-1928, ed. Description: 419 p. 22 cm. Subjects: Crusades. History. Variant Series: Essay index reprint LC Classification: D6 .C7 1968 Dewey Class No.: 940.1/8

The Crusades, and other historical essays; presented to Dana C. Munro by his former students. Edited by Louis J. Paetow. Published/Created: New York, F.S. Crofts 1928. Editors: Paetow, Louis John, 1880-1928, ed. Description: x, 419 p. frnt. (port.) 24 cm. Notes: "This edition is strictly limited to seven hundred and fifty copies printed from type, of which this is copy number 364." Bibliographical foot Subjects: Munro, Dana Carleton, 1866-1933. Crusades. History. LC Classification: D6 .C7 Dewey Class No.: 940.1/8

The Crusades, idea and reality, 1095-1274 / Louise and Jonathan Riley-Smith. Published/Created: London: E. Arnold, 1981. Editors: Riley-Smith, Louise. Riley-Smith, Jonathan Simon Christopher, 1938- Description: xiii, 191 p.: ill.; 24 cm. ISBN: 0713163488 (pbk.): Notes: Includes index. Bibliography: p. 178-181. Subjects: Crusades. Series: Documents of medieval history (London, England); 4. Series: Documents of medieval history; 4 LC Classification: D157 .C78 1981 Dewey Class No.: 909.07 19 Language Code: engmul

The first crusade: origins and impact / edited by Jonathan Phillips. Published/Created: Manchester, UK; New York, NY: Manchester University Press; New York, NY: Distributed exclusively in the USA by St. Martin's Press, 1997. Editors: Phillips, Jonathan (Jonathan P.) Description: xvi, 202 p.; 23 cm. ISBN: 0719049857 (cloth) 0719051746 (pbk.) Notes: Based on papers presented

at the London Centre for the
Study of the Crusades conference
"Deus Vult: The Origins and
Impact of the First Crusade", held
at the Institute of Historical
Research, London, 11-25-1995.
Includes bibliographical
references (p. [189]-192) and
index.
Subjects: Crusades--First, 1096-
1099--Congresses.
LC Classification: D161.2 .F54
1997
Dewey Class No.: 956/.014 21

The First Crusade: the chronicle of
Fulcher of Chartres and other
source materials / edited by
Edward Peters.
Edition Information: 2nd ed.
Published/Created: Philadelphia:
University of Pennsylvania Press,
c1998.
Editors: Peters, Edward, 1936-
Description: xiv, 317 p.; 24 cm.
ISBN: 0812216563 (paper: alk.
paper)
Notes: Includes bibliographical
references.
Subjects: Crusades--First, 1096-
1099--Sources.
Series: Middle Ages
Series
LC Classification: D161.1 .F57
1998
Dewey Class No.: 940.1/8 21

The holy war: [papers] / edited by
Thomas Patrick Murphy.
Published/Created: Columbus:
Ohio State University Press,
c1976.
Editors: Murphy, Thomas
Patrick. Ohio. State University,
Columbus. Center for Medieval
and Renaissance Studies.
Description: viii, 214 p.: ill.; 23
cm.
ISBN: 0814202454:
Notes: Sponsored by the Ohio
State University's Center for
Medieval and Renaissance
Studies. Includes bibliographical
references and index.
Subjects: Crusades--Congresses.
LC Classification: D160 .C66
1974

The Jews and the Crusaders: the
Hebrew chronicles of the first and
second Crusades / translated and
edited by Shlomo Eidelberg.
Published/Created: Hoboken,
N.J.: KTAV Pub. House, 1996.
Editors: Eidelberg, Shlomo,
1918-
Description: xi, 186 p.: ill., maps;
22 cm.
ISBN: 0881255416
Notes: Previously published:
Madison, Wis.: University of
Wisconsin Press, 1977. Includes
bibliographical references and
index.

Subjects: Jews--Germany--History--1096-1147--Sources. Civilization, Medieval--Jewish influences--Sources. Jews--Persecutions--Germany--Sources. Crusades--First, 1096-1099--Sources. Crusades--Second, 1147-1149--Sources. Germany--History--843-1273--Sources.
LC Classification: DS135.G31 J48 1996
Dewey Class No.: 943/.09424 20
Language Code: eng heb

The Jews and the Crusaders: the Hebrew chronicles of the First and Second Crusades / translated and edited by Shlomo Eidelberg.
Published/Created: Madison: University of Wisconsin Press, 1977.
Editors: Eidelberg, Shlomo, 1918-
Description: xii, 186 p.: ill.; 23 cm.
ISBN: 0299070603:
Notes: Includes bibliographical references and index.
Subjects: Jews--Germany--History--1096-1147--Sources. Jews--Persecutions--Germany--Sources. Crusades--First, 1096-1099--Sources. Crusades--Second, 1147-1149--Sources. Germany--History--843-1273--Sources.
LC Classification: DS135.G31

J48
Dewey Class No.: 943/.004/924
Language Code: engheb

The Jérusalem continuations.
Published/Created: University: University of Alabama Press, c1984-<1987
Description: v. <1-2: ill.; 25 cm.
Incomplete
Notes: Old French text, English commentary. Includes index.
Bibliography: pt. 1, p. [lxiii]-lxvii; pt. 2, p. [xlvix]-liii.
Subjects: Crusades--Romances. Chansons de geste. Epic poetry, French. French poetry--To 1500.
Series: The Old French crusade cycle; v. 7
LC Classification: PQ1311 .O43 vol. 7, etc.
Dewey Class No.: 841/.03 s 841/.03 19
Language Code: engfro

The Jérusalem continuations: the London-Turin version / edited by Peter R. Grillo.
Published/Created: Tuscaloosa: University of Alabama Press, c1994.
Editors: Grillo, Peter R., 1940-
Description: 1057 p., [2] leaves of plates: ill.; 25 cm.
ISBN: 0817307613 (alk. paper)
Notes: Text in Old French, introduction and commentary in

English. Includes bibliographical references.
Subjects: Crusades--Romances.
Chansons de geste. Epic poetry, French. French poetry--To 1500.
Series: The Old French Crusade cycle; v. 8
LC Classification: PQ1311 .O43 vol. 8
Dewey Class No.: 841/.1 20
Language Code: froeng

The Meeting of two worlds: cultural exchange between East and West during the period of the Crusades / editor, Vladimir P. Goss, associate editor, Christine Verzór Bornstein.
Published/Created: Kalamazoo, Mich.: Medieval Institute Publications, Western Michigan University, 1986.
Editors: Goss, Vladimir P. Bornstein, Christine Verzór. Michigan Consortium for Medieval and Early Modern Studies. University of Michigan. Medieval and Renaissance Collegium. Western Michigan University. Medieval Institute.
Description: 450 p., [73] p. of plates: ill., maps, plans; 24 cm.
ISBN: 0918720583 0918720591 (pbk.)
Notes: English, French, and Italian. Papers from a symposium sponsored by the Michigan

Consortium for Medieval and Early Modern Studies, the Medieval and Renaissance Collegium of the University of Michigan, and the Medieval Institute of Western Michigan University. Includes bibliographies.
Subjects: East and West--Congresses. Crusades--Influence--Congresses.
Series: Studies in medieval culture; 21
LC Classification: CB351 .S83 vol. 21 CB251
Dewey Class No.: 303.4/821811/01812 19
Language Code: engfreita

The Old French Crusade cycle / general editors, Jan A. Nelson, Emanuel J. Mickel.
Published/Created: Tuscaloosa: University of Alabama Press, c1977-
Editors: Nelson, Jan. Mickel, Emanuel J., 1937- Myers, Geoffrey M.
Description: v. <1-6; 7, pt. 1-2; 8-10: ill.; 25 cm.
ISBN: 0817385010 (v. 1)
Notes: Vol. 1 includes an essay on the mss. of the cycle by G. M. Myers.
Subjects: Crusades--Romances. Knights and knighthood--Poetry. French poetry--To 1500.

Chansons de geste.
LC Classification: PQ1311 .O43
Dewey Class No.: 841/.03 19
Language Code: engfro

The Oxford history of the Crusades /
    edited by Jonathan Riley-Smith.
Published/Created: Oxford; New
York: Oxford University Press,
c1999.
Editors: Riley-Smith, Jonathan
Simon Christopher, 1938-
Description: x, 457 p.: ill., maps;
20 cm.
ISBN: 0192853643
Notes: Originally published: The
Oxford illustrated history of the
Crusades, 1995. Includes
bibliographical references (p.
[402]-415) and index.
Subjects: Crusades.
LC Classification: D157 .O48
1999
Dewey Class No.: 909.7 21

The Oxford illustrated history of the
    Crusades / edited by Jonathan
Riley-Smith. Portion of
Illustrated history of the Crusades
Published/Created: New York:
Oxford University Press, 1997.
Projected Pub. Date: 9705
Editors: Riley-Smith, Jonathan
Simon Christopher, 1938-
Description: p. cm.
ISBN: 0192852949
Notes: Includes index.

Subjects: Crusades.
LC Classification: D157 .O48
1997
Dewey Class No.: 909.07 21

The Oxford illustrated history of the
    Crusades / edited by Jonathan
Riley-Smith.
Published/Created: Oxford; New
York: Oxford University Press,
1995.
Editors: Riley-Smith, Jonathan
Simon Christopher, 1938-
Description: x, 436 p.: ill., maps;
26 cm.
ISBN: 0198204353
Notes: Includes bibliographical
references (p. [401]-408) and
index.
Subjects: Crusades.
LC Classification: D157 .O48
1995
Dewey Class No.: 909.7 20

The Second Crusade and the
    Cistercians / edited by Michael
Gervers.
Published/Created: New York:
St. Martin's Press, 1992.
Editors: Gervers, Michael, 1942-
Description: xxi, 266 p.: ill.,
maps; 22 cm.
ISBN: 0312056079
Notes: Includes bibliographical
references (p. [211]-253) and
index.
Subjects: Bernard, of Clairvaux,

Saint, 1090 or 91-1153. Cistercians. Crusades--Second, 1147-1149.
LC Classification: D162.2 .S43 1992
Dewey Class No.: 909.07 20

The Three kings' sons: part 1 / edited by F.J. Furnivall.
Published/Created: Millwood, N.Y.: Kraus Reprint, 1987.
Editors: Furnivall, Frederick James, 1825-1910. Aubert, David, fl. 1458-1479. British Library. Manuscript. Harley 326.
Description: vii, 216 p.; 22 cm.
ISBN: 0527002712:
Notes: Translation of: Les Trois fils de rois. Attributed to David Aubert. Edited from manuscript, Harleian 326, about 1500 A.D. Reprint. Originally published: London: Kegan Paul, Trench, Trubner, 1895. (Early English Text Society. Extra Series; 67). Includes index.
Subjects: Crusades--Romances. Epic literature, French--Translations into English.
Series: Early English Text Society (Series). Extra Series; 67.
LC Classification: PQ1581.T76 E5 1987
Dewey Class No.: 843/.2 19

Language Code: engfre

Throop, Palmer Allan, 1902-
Criticism of the crusade: a study of public opinion and crusade propoganda [by] Palmer A. Throop.
Published/Created: Amsterdam, N. v. Swets & Zeitlinger, 1940.
Description: xv, 291 p. 24 cm.
Notes: "In large part a reworking of a thesis accepted by Princeton university in 1934."--Pref.
Subjects: Crusades--Later, 13th, 14th, and 15th centuries.
LC Classification: D160 .T48 1940
Dewey Class No.: 940.18

Tolerance and intolerance: social conflict in the age of the Crusades / edited by Michael Gervers and James M. Powell.
Edition Information: 1st ed.
Published/Created: Syracuse, N.Y.: Syracuse University Press, 2001.
Editors: Gervers, Michael, 1942- Powell, James M.
Description: xx, 191 p.: ill.; 23 cm.
ISBN: 0815628692 (alk. paper) 0815628706 (pbk.: alk. paper)
Notes: Includes bibliographical references (p. 177-183) and index.
Subjects: Toleration--History--To

1500. Social conflict--History--To 1500. Religious tolerance--History--To 1500. Crusades.
Series: Medieval studies (Syracuse, N.Y.)
Variant Series: Medieval studies
LC Classification: HM1271 .T65 2001
Dewey Class No.: 303.3/85 21

Treece, Henry, 1911-1966.
Know about the Crusades.
Published/Created: [Chester Springs, Pa.] Dufour, 1967 [c1963]
Description: 62 p. illus. (part col.) 21 cm.
Notes: Bibliography: p. 62.
Subjects: Crusades--Juvenile literature.
LC Classification: D158 .T8
Dewey Class No.: 270.4

Trotter, D. A.
Medieval French literature and the crusades (1100-1300) / D.A. Trotter.
Published/Created: Genéve: Librairie Droz, 1988.
Description: 277 p.; 22 cm.
Notes: Slightly rev. ed. of the author's thesis (Ph. D.)--Oxford University. Bibliography: p. [251]-274.
Subjects: French literature--To 1500--History and criticism.
Crusades in literature. Epic literature, French--History and criticism. Chansons de geste--History and criticism.
Civilization, Medieval, in literature. Literature and history.
Series: Histoire des idées et critique littéraire; v. 256.
Variant Series: Histoire des idées et critique littéraire; vol. 256
LC Classification: PQ155.C86 T76 1988
Dewey Class No.: 840.9/358 20

Tryon, Rolla Milton, 1875- ed.
Crusading Europe, 1095-1291.
Published/Created: Indianapolis, G. F. Cram Co. [1954]
Editors: Cram (George F.) Company.
Description: col. map 88 x 127 cm.
Subjects: Crusades--Maps.
Europe--Historical geography--Maps.
LC Classification: G5701 .S33 1954.T7

Tyerman, Christopher.
England and the Crusades, 1095-1588 / Christopher Tyerman.
Published/Created: Chicago: University of Chicago Press, 1988.
Description: xvi, 492 p.: ill.; 24 cm.
ISBN: 0226820122:
Notes: Includes index.

Bibliography: p. 445-465.
Subjects: Crusades. Great Britain--History--Medieval period, 1066-1485. Great Britain--History--Tudors, 1485-1603. England--Church history--1066-1485. England--Church history--16th century.
LC Classification: DA176 .T94 1988
Dewey Class No.: 942 19

Tyerman, Christopher.
The invention of the Crusades / Christopher Tyerman.
Published/Created: Toronto; Buffalo: University of Toronto Press, 1998.
Description: ix, 170 p.; 23 cm.
ISBN: 0802043631 0802081851 (pbk.)
Notes: Includes bibliographical references (p. 158-161) and index.
Subjects: Crusades. Crusades--Historiography.
LC Classification: D160 .T94 1998
Dewey Class No.: 909.07 21

Usamah ibn Munqidh, 1095-1188.
An Arab-Syrian gentleman and warrior in the period of the Crusades: memoirs of Usamah ibn-Munqidh (Kitab al-I'tibar); translated from the original manuscript by Philip K. Hitti;

with a new foreword by Richard W. Bulliet.
Published/Created: New York: Columbia University Press, c2000.
Editors: Hitti, Philip Khuri, 1886-
Description: xv, 265 p.: ill., map; 24 cm.
ISBN: 0231121245 (cloth: alk. paper) 0231121253 (paper: alk. paper)
Notes: Includes bibliographical references and index.
Subjects: Usamah ibn Munqidh, 1095-1188. Crusades. Crusades--Personal narratives. Syria--History--750-1260.
Series: Records of Western civilization
LC Classification: DS97.3 .U813 2000
Dewey Class No.: 956.91/02 21
Language Code: eng ara

Usamah ibn Munqidh, 1095-1188.
The autobiography of OusBma.
Published/Created: London, G. Routledge & sons, ltd., 1929.
Editors: Potter, G. R. (George Richard), 1900- tr.
Description: 301 p.
Subjects: Crusades. Syria--History.
Variant Series: Broadway medieval library
LC Classification: DS97 .U7

Language Code: engfreara

Villehardouin, Geoffroi de, d. ca. 1212.
Memoirs of the crusades / by Villehardouin & de Joinville; translated by Sir Frank Marzials.
Published/Created: Westport, Conn.: Greenwood Press, 1983.
Editors: Joinville, Jean, sire de, 1224?-1317?.
Description: xli, [1], 340 p.; 23 cm.
ISBN: 0313238561 (lib. bdg.)
Notes: Reprint. Originally published: London: J.M. Dent; New York: E.P. Dutton, 1908. (Everyman's library. History; no. 333) Includes index. Bibliography: p. [xlii]
Subjects: Louis IX, King of France, 1214-1270. Villehardouin, Geoffroi de, d. ca. 1212. Joinville, Jean, sire de, 1224?-1317?. Crusades--Fourth, 1202-1204 Crusades--Seventh, 1248-1250. Istanbul (Turkey)-- History. Latin Empire, 1204-1261.
LC Classification: D164.A3 V53 1983
Dewey Class No.: 940.1/84 19

West, Anthony, 1914-
All about the Crusades / Anthony West; illustrated by Carl Rose.
Published/Created: London:

W.H. Allen, 1967.
Description: 185 p.: col. ill., col. maps; 23 cm.
Subjects: Crusades.
LC Classification: D158 .W4 1967

West, Anthony, 1914-
The Crusades; illustrated by Carl Rose.
Published/Created: New York, Random House [1954]
Description: 185 p. illus. 22 cm.
Subjects: Crusades.
Variant Series: World landmark books, W-11
LC Classification: D158 .W4
Dewey Class No.: 940.18

William, of Tyre, Archbishop of Tyre, ca. 1130-ca. 1190.
A history of deeds done beyond the sea, by William, archbishop of Tyre ... Translated and annotated by Emily Atwater Babcock and A. C. Krey.
Published/Created: New York, Columbia University Press, 1943.
Editors: Babcock, Emily Atwater, ed. and tr. Krey, August C. (August Charles), 1887-1961, ed.
Description: 2 v. maps (1 fold.) 24 cm.
Notes: Translation of Historia rerum in partibus transmarinis gestarum. "The edition of William's history used as the

basis of this translation is that prepared by A. Beugnot and A. Le Prevost for the French academy ... The present translation has been done by Mrs. Babcock."--Introd., v. 1, p. 44.
Bibliography: v. 2, p. [511]-520.
Subjects: Crusades. Jerusalem--History--Latin Kingdom, 1099-1244.
Series: Records of civilization, sources and studies, no. 35
LC Classification: D152 .G78
Dewey Class No.: 940.18
Language Code: englat

William, of Tyre, Archbishop of Tyre, ca. 1130-ca. 1190.
A Middle English chronicle of the First Crusade: the Caxton Eracles / [edited by] Dana Cushing.
Published/Created: Lewiston, N.Y.: Mellen Press, 2001.
Projected Pub. Date: 1111
Editors: Cushing, Dana.
Description: p. cm.
ISBN: 0773474250 (v. 1) 0773474277 (v. 2)
Notes: Translation of the 1st nine books of the Historia rerum in partibus transmarinis gestarum. Includes bibliographical references and index.
Subjects: Godfrey, of Bouillon, ca. 1060-1100. Crusades--First, 1096-1099--Sources. English

language--Middle English, 1100-1500--Texts. Military art and science--Europe--History--To 1500 Sources. Military art and science--Islamic Empire--History Sources. Jerusalem--History--Latin Kingdom, 1099-1244--Sources. Europe--History, Military--Sources.
Series: Texts and studies in religion; v. 88.
Variant Series: Text and studies in religion; 88
LC Classification: D183.3 .W55213 2001
Dewey Class No.: 940.1/8 21
Language Code: engenm frmenm

William, of Tyre, Archbishop of Tyre, ca. 1130-ca. 1190.
The history of Godefrey of Boloyne and of the conquest of Iherusalem.
Published/Created: [Hammersmith: Kelmscott Press, 1893]
Editors: Caxton, William, ca. 1422-1491. Sparling, H. Halliday (Henry Halliday) Morris, William, 1834-1896. Kelmscott Press.
Description: xxii, 450 p.; 30 cm.
Notes: "This new edition of William Caxton's Godeffroy of Boloyne, done after the first edition, was corrected for the press by H. Halliday Sparling,

and printed by me, William
Morris, at the Kelmscott Press ...
Hammersmith ... 1893"--
Colophon. References: Peterson,
W.S. Kelmscott Press A15
Subjects: Godfrey, of Bouillon,
ca. 1060-1100. Crusades--First,
1096-1099. Jerusalem--History--
Latin Kingdom, 1099-1244.
LC Classification: D152 .G783
1893
Language Code: eng frelat

Williams, Jay, 1914-
Knights of the crusades, by the
editors of Horizon magazine. Jay
Williams in consultation with
Margaret B. Freeman.
Edition Information: 1st ed.
Published/Created: New York,
American Heritage Pub. Co.;
book trade distribution by
Meredith Press, c1962.
Description: 153 p. illus. 27 cm.
Subjects: Crusades--Juvenile
literature. Knights and
knighthood--History--To 1500--
Juvenile literature.
Variant Series: A Horizon caravel
book
LC Classification: D158 .W5
Dewey Class No.: 940.1

Wise, Terence.
Armies of the Crusades / text by
Terence Wise; colour plates by
G. A. Embleton.

Published/Created: London:
Osprey Pub., 1978.
Editors: Embleton, G. A. (Gerry
A.)
Description: 40 p., [4] leaves of
plates: ill. (some col.); 25 cm.
ISBN: 0850451256
Subjects: Armies--History.
Crusades. Military art and
science--History. Military
history, Medieval.
Variant Series: Men-at-arms
Series
LC Classification: U37 .W54
Dewey Class No.: 355/.009/033

World history illustrated. III. Middle
Ages [computer file]. Portion of
Middle Ages
Edition Information: Macintosh
version.
Published/Created: Fairfield, CT:
Queue, c1994.
Editors: Queue, Inc.
Description: 1 computer laser
optical disc; 4 3/4 in. + 1 guide.
Computer File Info.: Computer
data and programs. Macintosh
System 6.0.7 CD-ROM drive
Notes: Title from disc label.
Issued also for MS-DOS CD-
ROM platform. System
requirements: Macintosh; 2MB
RAM; System 6.0.7 or better;
color monitor; CD-ROM drive.
Word processing software
required to view some

supplemental material.
Subjects: Middle Ages--History--
Databases. Civilization, Ancient--
Databases. Europe--History--476-
1492--Databases.
LC Classification: D117
Dewey Class No.: 940.1 12

World history illustrated. III. Middle
Ages [computer file]. Portion of
Middle Ages
Edition Information: MS-DOS
CD-ROM [version].
Published/Created: Fairfield, CT:
Queue, c1994.
Editors: Queue, Inc.
Description: 1 computer laser
optical disc; 4 3/4 in. + 1 guide.
Computer File Info.: Computer
data and programs. PC MS-DOS
CD-ROM drive
Notes: Title from disc label.
Issued also for Macintosh
platform. System requirements:
PC; 640KB RAM; MS-DOS;
MCGA or VGA monitor; hard
disk with 500KB free space; CD-
ROM drive. Sound blaster card
required for audio play.
Subjects: Middle Ages--History--
Databases. Civilization, Ancient--
Databases. Europe--History--476-
1492--Databases.
LC Classification: D117
Dewey Class No.: 940.1 12

Yonge, Charlotte Mary, 1823-1901.
The prince and the page; a story
of the last crusade, by Charlotte
M. Yonge; illustrations by
Marguerite de Angeli.
Published/Created: New York,
The Macmillan Company, 1925.
Description: vii p., 3 l., 246 p.
incl. illus., plates. col. front.,
plates (part col.) 20 cm.
Subjects: Crusades--Eighth,
1270--Fiction.
LC Classification: PZ3.Y8 Pr10

Zachariadou, Elisavet A.
Trade and crusade: Venetian
Crete and the Emirates of
Menteshe and Aydin (1300-1415)
/ Elizabeth A. Zachariadou.
Published/Created: Venice:
Istituto ellenico di studi bizantini
e postbizantini di Venezia per
tutti i paesi del mondo, 1983.
Description: xxxvi, 270 p.: ill.;
24 cm.
Notes: English, Greek, and Latin.
Title on added t.p.: Emporio kai
staurophoria. Includes
bibliographical references (p.
[xiv]-xxvii) and index.
Subjects: Commerce--History--
Medieval, 500-1500. Crusades.
Crete (Greece)--History--
Venetian rule, 1204-1669. Venice
(Italy)--History--697-1508.
Venice (Italy)--Foreign relations.
Mediterranean Region--Church

history. Crete (Greece)--
Commerce--Turkey. Turkey--
Commerce--Greece--Crete.
Series: Bibliothéque de l'Institut
hellénique d'études byzantines et
post-byzantines de Venise; no
11.
Variant Series: Library of the
Hellenic Institute of Byzantine
and Post-Byzantine Studies; no.
11
LC Classification: DF901.C83
Z34 1983
Language Code: enggrelat